Winter Watch

Winter Watch

by
James Ramsey

Illustrations by
Laura Dassow

Alaska Northwest Books™
Anchorage • Edmonds

Library of Congress Cataloging-in-Publication Data

Ramsey, James, 1929-
    Winter Watch / by James Ramsey ; illustrated by Laura Dassow
      p. cm.
    ISBN 0-88240-329-X
    1. Alaska – Social life and customs. 2. Winter – Alaska.
   3. Ramsey, James, 1929- –Diaries. I. Title.
   F910.5.R36 1989
   979.8'705'0924–dc19
   [B]

Cover and book design by David Berger

Alaska Northwest Books™
A Division of GTE Discovery Publications, Inc.

130 2nd Ave. S., Edmonds, WA 98020

Printed in U.S.A

For Zachary, welcome!

 Contents

Foreword

Above the Arctic Circle in northwest Alaska is a little-known region of great natural beauty and stark solitude known as the Schwatka Mountains. The Schwatkas are part of the Brooks Range, which stretches across the top of Alaska from the Chukchi Sea to the Canadian border. It is the northernmost chain of mountains on this planet.

Northwest Alaska is wild and desolate. There are no roads, and very few people. South of the Schwatkas are a few scattered Eskimo villages, usually at the mouths of rivers that break free from the mountains, flow across the flat Arctic tundra, and end their brief but spectacular lives where they join the Kobuk River. Deep in the mountains, near the rivers, are a few log cabins and sod igloos built more than a decade ago when the land was opened by the State to anyone who had the courage and tenacity to go up there and prove out a five-acre parcel of land.

On the bank of one of these rivers, upstream of the tundra, enveloped by mountains, is a small one-room log cabin hidden in a grove of spruce. It is forty miles from the nearest Eskimo village, and a lot farther than that, by any measurement, from the chaos and confusion of modern urban life. There is nothing special or pretentious about this particular cabin, except perhaps to those who built it or lived in it. I am one of those who lived in it. For nine months, from September to June, this cabin was my Arctic classroom, where I learned the taste and touch, the sound and smell and sight of an Arctic winter.

What follows is a somewhat bemused account of that sometimes mystifying, occasionally frightening and, in retrospect, altogether glorious time. This is not a work of fiction, although at times it may seem so. The locale and the river are real. I do not name them because it is my belief that each one of us should have the chance to experience the joy of discovering, as I did, his own magic place.

September

Day 1, September 15

Word came last night that we were "go" for the Arctic. The word was a message from Mike Schieber that he had marked out a landing site with ribbons on a river bar about a half-mile above my chosen winter residence, a small log cabin located in the north-western Brooks Range above the Arctic Circle. Mike was to be my nearest and for a time only neighbor within forty miles. He had gone up there early, before freeze-up, to set up a fish camp where he hoped to catch enough fish to feed his sled dogs through the coming winter.

I had wanted to get closer to the land, and at fifty-three I felt I had been getting sloppy, physically, mentally, and spiritually. A test of some kind seemed to be in order and upon hearing that a cabin — unlived in for the past several years — in one of the last great wildernesses on earth, was available just for the asking, I jumped at the chance. Well, not exactly "jumped." As a matter of fact I waffled most of the summer, one day going, the next not, until finally forced to decide by the rapidly approaching end of summer.

This morning when I arrived at the charter flight office at the Fairbanks airport — I had unloaded about one thousand pounds of food and gear there the day before — the place was crowded with pilots and passengers getting ready, as I was, to fly out into the bush. The size of the crowd reinforced what I already knew: If you travel north from Fairbanks you go by air. My pilot and aircraft, a Helio STOL (short take-off and landing) were out on an early morning run and due back at nine. While I waited, sitting on a couple of boxes of my groceries, I tried to imagine what I had forgotten, because the single biggest challenge I faced in preparing for an Arctic winter was compiling a nine-month grocery list.

When my pilot arrived we loaded my supplies on board — they filled every inch of cargo space — and then began to discuss our destination. There was no problem with finding the right river. The pilot had good aerial maps for that. But finding the cabin was something else. All the help I had for that was a little hand-drawn map which showed a trio of cabins about a mile from one another, two on the river and one on a nearby lake. At the base of the triangle of cabins, and across the river, was the landing site, and nearby, according to Mike, would be a canoe. As the pilot was topping off the fuel tanks I could hear him muttering to himself about longitudes, latitudes, and *real* maps.

As soon as we were in the air the pilot metamorphosed from a grouch into a friendly person, partly, I thought, because he was now in his own element. He asked a lot of questions about why I wanted to winter in the Brooks Range, but I don't think he understood my somewhat tentative answers any more than I did. I was just beginning to comprehend the enormity of what I was about to do. I was going to let this man beside me land me on a river bar many miles from any kind of civilization, and he was going to leave me there, *alone*. There would be no welcoming committee: Mike would be quite a few miles downstream at his fish camp for the next several weeks.

We landed at the little community of Bettles to top off the fuel tanks. While there I purchased from the trading post two bananas — possibly my last fresh fruit for eight months — a can of black olives, and a pair of wool gloves, the latter an indication of my mental state because I already had about ten pairs. I was beginning to feel a little panic.

Later, after we had paralleled the magnificent southern slopes of the Brooks Range, the pilot pointed out the river in the distance, flowing south, and said that was the one we wanted. We were going to turn north and follow the river into the mountains. As we lost altitude the mountains on each side of the river rose around us. A few tense minutes later I spotted a cabin near a small lake. "I've got a cabin on the right and a small lake," I yelled just as we flashed over another cabin and a tall food cache on the east bank of the river. "If there is another cabin on that promontory coming up, this must be the place." The pilot nodded and then said, "There is a canoe down below me, and there's your third cabin. Let's go down and look for ribbon." He laid the plane over on its wingtip in a tight turn. The ribbons were not all that easy to see, but they were there, delineating a small river bar of fairly level gravel and rock. We made one more turn while the pilot studied the terrain. Then he cranked out all the flaps, turned into the final approach, cut the throttle, and with a lot of noise and bouncing around we came to a stop with a couple of hundred feet to spare. No matter how this adventure eventually turns out I will always be proud of my next statement: "Piece of cake," I said as I clicked open my seat belt. He looked at me rather oddly, then smiled and said, "Well, I suppose you want this stuff unloaded."

Soon, too soon, I was thinking, the pilot wished me luck — luck? What kind of wish was that? He blasted into the air like a rocket and rapidly vanished to the south. I pivoted slowly, hearing now only the sound of the river flowing, and looked north. There in the foreground was this pitifully small pile of apple cartons, a pair of snowshoes, a .30-30 lever-action rifle, and a portable typewriter. That was all. In the background, looming is the only proper word, was the Brooks Range. Jim, I thought to myself, is it possible that you may have committed a tactical error?

I didn't really panic at that point — I have been alone before — but I suddenly felt compelled to do everything *now*. Even though it was only eleven in the morning with at least eight hours of daylight left. The urgency came from being on the wrong side of the river from my cabin. However irrational that was, I knew that was what was bothering me. I didn't like the feeling of being isolated from what I then thought of as my warm, snug little cabin.

So I dragged the canoe, a big aluminum Grumman, from its willow berth, paddled it down to my supplies, loaded half of them, and headed for the cabin a half-mile away.

The cabin looked just like the photos I had seen. It was made from spruce logs with a sod roof, and had a profile so low that it appeared to have sunk into the ground. It was completely closed up, with anti-bear shutters bristling with outward-facing nails covering each of the three small windows. I opened the storm door which led into a small entryway, and then opened the door into the cabin's interior. I stepped into pitch darkness. The light from my small flashlight was swallowed whole. My nostrils were immediately assailed by fetid, moist odors of decay and rot. It was what I had always imagined a grizzly bear den would smell like at the end of a long winter! My feet were slipping on a surface that was wet and covered with what later turned out to be rotting paper and cloth. Every surface I touched was slimy.

I was about to back out of this dank catastrophe when my groping hands encountered something familiar; a glass chimney, and below that the squat form of an old-fashioned kerosene lantern. I shook it gently and heard liquid gurgle. I searched for my matches, not really believing the lamp would light after all this time. But it did, after six years *lux sit!* The place was better in darkness. Then, I had to deal only with touch and smell. Now, I could see the extent of the disaster. The floor was awash with liquid muck. The roof dripped water. Mildew was on every surface and every object in sight. I touched a piece of caribou fur covering a small chair, and it turned to mush in my hand. So, I thought distractedly, the challenge of the Arctic is not trying to keep from freezing to death, but, rather, avoiding being eviscerated by massive doses of jungle rot.

Backing away from this miniature Armageddon, I determined to get my priorities straight: First, the supplies, then the cabin. There was no way I could put the first canoe load in the cabin — it would rot while I was getting the second — so I decided to stack it in a small workshop which had a separate entrance but was attached to one end of the cabin.

Having retrieved the remaining supplies and stored all the gear in the workshop, I faced the interior of the cabin for the second time. First I removed the anti-bear shutters, which provided a lot more light. But alas, more light only illuminated more misery. Rows of rotting work gloves hung along a roof pole; pot holders, green with mildew, hung neatly from nails; a foam-rubber mattress was torn into a thousand bits and arranged into an orderly (or, so I supposed) squirrel nest. There were other nests, one on top of the cupboard, and one on what appeared to have been a bookshelf.

The wood stove, for cooking and heating, sat somewhat forlornly off to one side of the room, rusting quietly away not far from an equally rusty stovepipe sticking down through the roof.

A warm fire, I thought, is the only answer to this moist miasma. I hooked up the stove, emptied about fifty pounds of ashes and assorted wet gunk from its gut, and began raping nearby spruce trees of their dead branches in lieu of the presence of one single dry piece of wood within the cabin. And, like the old kerosene lantern, lo, there was fire.

With the fire going things began looking up, but the job of cleaning up was still formidable. The real turning point came when I discovered the only usable cleaning tool in the cabin: a twig broom. I have spent many enjoyable months in Greece without ever seeing a real broom. And yet every Greek home I have visited has always been spotless. To hell with it, I thought, if they can do it, so can I. And I did.

Late at night I crawled wearily into bed and slid gratefully down between my blanket sheets. As my eyes were closing, drops of water began to fall sporadically on the bedclothes. Without even thinking, I reached behind me, grabbed my rain parka, spread it out like a bedspread, and buried myself beneath it. Welcome to the semi-frozen Arctic, I said to myself as I drifted off.

Day 2, September 16 (Low 36, High 55, cloudy)

Still operating under a compulsive need to get things done fast, I scurried about the cabin cleaning, sweeping and arranging (and rearranging) foodstuffs. The basic problem was storage. There was, to be sure, a beautiful food cache—a small cabinlike structure perched on log piling about twenty feet above the ground — supposedly impervious to all creatures from tiny lemmings to huge grizzly bears. But when I leaned a ladder up to its door and climbed up to look, I found it crammed to the ceiling with clothing, caribou pelts, a whole miscellany of items left behind by the cabin's owner six years ago. It was practically an elevated archaeological dig in that sense, but there was no room for my food.

There was a full-size aluminum garbage can with lid that was only about one-third full of flour, dried potatoes and a few other items. I hauled that down into the cabin and filled it with my flour, sugar, beans, pancake mix, etcetera. The canned goods were no problem as they could withstand both animals and cold.

By late afternoon there was a dim glow at the end of the tunnel, metaphorically speaking. The cabin was beginning to feel livable. There was still the problem of water dripping down from the ceiling, not just over the bed but, sporadically, all over. I had made the bed "rain proof" by tacking a canopy of Visqueen over it, but I could hardly do that for the whole cabin! Besides, in the long run, I was beginning to think such a move was self-defeating. I had thought the roof was leaking. Now I began to think otherwise, for I noticed that each time I had a fire in the stove really throwing out heat the "leaks" would increase. I began to think of the cabin as an enormous cloud chamber. Because it had been unoccupied for several years, and hence no fires to dry it out, the floor accumulated a tremendous amount of moisture, enough to almost ruin it. Now that I was firing up the stove, the moisture was trying to escape. But as the warm, moist air rose to the ceiling it encountered the plastic Visqueen that had been laid over the rafters before putting on the sod roof. The moist air was condensing on the underside of the Visqueen. I was making my own rain storms. Or, at least so I reasoned. I vowed to keep a fire going until the whole cabin was finally dry.

The positive motivating force today, like the discovery of the "Greek" twig broom of yesterday, came from my invention of the "E-Z Rest Outdoor Privy Harness." This may require some explanation. The outdoor toilet here, I discovered, is a simple slit trench covered with a few boards for sanitation and to keep it from filling with snow. This is not much different from the "squatters" one encounters in France and much of the rest of Europe. But I have difficulty with this whole genre of loos, because of a back that refuses to operate efficiently in the mandatory configuration. In European civilization I usually have to look for a water pipe or something to hang onto under the threat of falling backward. No such thing here, I soon discovered. So I began a quest.

I had not looked long when I found a harness for pulling a plastic sled over the snow. In the winter, both water and wood are hauled this way. If you don't have sled dogs, you make a harness for yourself and you do the pulling. And that is what this harness was, a simple waist harness made from two old padded backpack straps with a seat-beltlike catch to connect around your waist. From this waist belt was a strong strap about seven feet long which ended in a carabiner, a mountain-climbing catch which could be snapped open to hook onto the sled. But I saw other possibilities. What if the belt were turned backward so the strap led away from in front rather than behind? Then if there were a convenient tree about six or seven feet in front of the privy, the carabiner could be passed around the trunk and snapped back on its own lanyard. The subject would then be in a reverse three-point stance (two feet and the waist belt) suspended half-mast, as it were, over the privy (look ma, no hands!) in some degree of comfort.

Fortunately, sometime around the mid-twentieth century, a spruce seed had germinated approximately six-and-one-half feet due south of the privy, and the resulting tree had no doubt been waiting patiently for me to show up. *Voila!* It worked to perfection.

After two days in the cabin, and a fairly thorough search of the food cache, I had not been able to discover one single knife, fork or spoon. I was eating with my Swiss army knife. Tonight as I was chopping kindling inside the cabin for tomorrow's fire, I hit the floor rather hard with a particularly stubborn piece of wood. When I did so, a fork fell out of the sky, or so it seemed. On closer inspection I realized that the silverware drawer had been disguised to look like a matching wood carving at the top of the cabinet. Like most other things in the cabin, the cardboard bottom of the drawer had nearly rotted away from the excess moisture, and my slamming at the wood had jarred it loose. As I watched, spoons and knives followed until I had place settings for three or four people.

Day 3, September 17 (Low 33, High 50, light rain and snow)
More cleaning and food arranging. I began looking for wood for fuel. There is enough for about a week around the cabin, but I won't feel comfortable until I have at least two cords stacked and ready to burn. The floor is just today beginning to dry, but I think it will take another week before the taste, smell and feel of mildew leaves this place. I'm keeping a fire going about eighteen hours a day, even though the outside temperature doesn't warrant it.

Day 4, September 18 (Low 32, High 50, cloudy)
This evening at dusk when I went out to throw out the

dishwater, I followed my usual habit of walking the few extra feet to the point where I can see up and down the river for a mile or more. As I stepped out onto the point a caribou cow and two calves stared at me from just across a channel about fifty yards away. It was cold and I turned to fetch a jacket, thinking the caribou wouldn't spook. But my sudden movement frightened the cow and she and the calves made a great watery thrashing as they turned and swam through another channel heading down-river. When they reached *their* safe distance they stopped and began browsing on willow shrubs, leaving me unnoticed, forgotten, and just a trifle lonely.

Day 5, September 19 (Low 32, High 50, sunny)

Two things (among many others) have to be done before winter sets in. The sod has to be removed temporarily from the roof and a double sheet of six mil Visqueen laid down before the same sod is re-laid. The other job involves collecting moss for re-chinking the walls. The re-chinking can be done any time, but the moss must be collected and stored in a warm place before the first heavy freeze, which will make it too brittle to use.

Today I started on the roof. I'm going to do the east side of the roof first, carrying the squares of sod to the west side rather than to the ground and back up again; then I'll reverse the procedure, moving the roll of Visqueen around so it will eventually cover the entire roof without a break. This will be tricky! The work went well today even though it was slow and hard. But, of course, I'm not in shape yet, and "hard" for me may be "soft" for someone else.

I took a break at midday because of the nice weather and went off to explore the other two cabins. Mike is downriver at his fish camp so I knew both cabins would be empty. Mike's is about twice the size of mine and sits in a grove of coniferous and deciduous trees at the edge of a small lake. Nice setting but I like my river view better. His food cache is twice as big too, probably because he needs a lot of room to store feed for his sled-dog team. The other cabin sits on a spectacular bluff above the river about a mile north of my cabin. Its siting is too spectacular as it turns out. I was told earlier that it is so exposed out on the bluff, it is almost impossible to live in during winter. On this hike — the first time since I arrived that I have ventured very far from my cabin — I took my .30-30 along with me. I don't really know why.

Day 6, September 20 (Low 32, High 50, sunny)

I continued to work on the roof. Some of the sod comes up easily and in one piece. In other spots it is very crumbly and difficult to handle. In some places it is very thick, a foot or more, and therefore very, very heavy. I don't know whether what I am doing is right, but there seems to be more weight on the roof structure than is necessary, so I'm cutting it in half where it is really thick and tossing the remainder down to the ground.

Today was a day of "firsts." I saw the first aircraft since the one that brought me. The plane flew upriver and returned about twenty minutes later. It was high enough so I didn't bother waving. When I made one of my frequent visits to the point to check the river (it was still there) I saw my first fish swimming languidly in the big eddy. I don't know what it was, but it appeared to be about eighteen to twenty inches long, gray body, white belly. From what I have read it was probably a shee fish or Arctic grayling.

Also today I baked my first cake here. It was also the first time I have baked without the benefit of an oven. Here's how you do it! You need two items not normally associated with baking — a trivet, and a five-gallon rectangular can with one side cut out of it. You mix whatever you are baking — in this case devils food cake — put it in the pan, set it on a trivet on top of the stove, and cover it with the cut-out can. The can becomes the oven. The cake was slightly burned on the bottom but otherwise good. I'm doing this without a cooking thermometer so I imagine perfection will require practice.

Day 7, September 21 (Low 32, High 50, clear and sunny)

This morning, literally, the bottom fell out of my stove, and I began to wonder whether, figuratively, this didn't signal the bottom falling out of my winter in the Arctic! I repaired it, so to speak, but I do not think the stove can make it through the winter. It has been sitting here for the past half-dozen years, rusting away each summer. I knew it was in bad shape and had brought some stove cement to patch it, but given its condition that's like trying to save the *Titanic* with a wine cork.

I'll just have to wait until Mike shows up, maybe next week, maybe a month from now. Maybe he will know how to repair it somewhat permanently. Maybe we can go into the village and buy a new one. Maybe. I almost took the canoe downriver to discuss it with Mike, but I still have the roof to finish and the moss to chink. I don't really know what the priorities are in this case, which leaves a very large cloud of indecision hanging over this little cabin.

In any event, this is what I did for the short term. The stove is barrel-shaped with one side of the barrel cut out and replaced with a flat piece of metal for a cooking surface. It sits on legs on its side. The bottom one-third of the barrel is very, very rusty, but I didn't realize how rusty until this morning when two hand-sized pieces fell to the floor along with ashes and hot coals. No patch that I could think of would deal with that, so I began thinking more in terms of a crutch or a cast, a prosthesis, as it were.

I remembered seeing several unused pieces of stovepipe, the kind that is open along its length. When you wish to use it you close it by pushing the two edges together until they lock in place. But I wanted them open, very open. I took two three-foot lengths — the stove is about two inches longer than three feet — put them together, and bent them into the shape of the stove. These became the new bottom of the stove.

Then I went to the river and got a bucket of sand, which I put to a depth of several inches over the new "bottom." The sand served the dual purpose of holding the stovepipe in place by its weight, and insulating the thin stovepipe from the direct heat of the fire. I was concerned that the holes in the old bottom, now somewhat plugged but by no means airtight, would act as a draft which I couldn't control.

So I took a third length of pipe, spread it to match the outside contour of the stove bottom, and fitted it to the bottom, held in place by two empty honey tins which in height exactly matched the distance between the bottom of the stove and the floor. Then I built a fire and stood back to observe. So far it works (S.F.I.W.).

This afternoon I finished the first half of the roof job.

Day 8, September 22 (Low 20, High 32, clear)
As to the stove: S.F.I.W. The temperature did not get above

freezing today. The sod is like concrete. The roof job will have to wait.

Mike left a leg of caribou hanging in my food cache before he went to his fish camp. I've been cutting off a steak almost every night. To date, I have enjoyed Boo steak, Teriyaki Boo steak, Pepper Boo steak, and Garlic Boo steak, all good.

Baked brownies without burning them!

Day 9, September 23 (Low 20, High 30, clear)

The stove status is still S.F.I.W. Too cold again to work on the roof. I'm at a temporary impasse on the moss chinking operation. Before this present cold snap I collected six big plastic garbage bags of moss and am keeping them in the cabin under the bed as protection against freezing. I took a good look at the old chinking today and it looks very good. The moss is in between the logs like concrete, but there is a bit of Arctic technical information that I'm not privy to. It's embodied in the following question: Does moss, after a few years. lose its ability to insulate?

If it does, then I should tear it all out and replace it. If it doesn't, then except for a few spots I have already repaired, the cabin is in excellent shape moss-wise. It's not just a question of laziness. If it needs to be done I'll do it. But I'm not sure I can do as good a job as is apparently already done. I have decided to do a modified waffle. I'll wait until the roof is finished and if Mike has not shown up by then, I will go ahead and redo the whole nine yards, as they say. (He is not aware of it, at this point, but poor Michael is in danger of becoming a kind of Arctic guru in my mind.)

Day 10, September 24 (Low 20, High 32, clear)

Still no work on the roof. I did a lot of inside stuff today like sewing a rip in a pair of wool Dutch army pants, one of two pairs I bought at a surplus store in Fairbanks. They are actually too warm to wear in these present above-zero temperatures. There was no pillow nor pillowcase here and I didn't bring any, so today I found a bag of batting material, wrapped some cloth around it, and sewed it together. It looks like a pillow with pillowcase, but it certainly doesn't feel like one.

I also read for several hours. Prior to now I have never really kept a record of books I have read. But, since this is a journey

purported to be involved in an investigation of both mind and matter, I have decided to make a list of books and authors as I finish them. It will be found at the end of the journal. (Who am I writing this for? That last sentence reads as if I expect someone to find these notes adjacent to a neat mound of bones!)

Day 11, September 25 (Low 20*, High 32, clear)
   *These temps are taken usually first thing in the morning. It is no doubt several degrees colder at two or three in the morning.

   Three days ago, when this cold spell started, it was heralded by a change in the direction of the wind. Instead of coming upriver (from the south) it came swirling downriver (from the north) straight out of the Brooks Range. It carried along with it a load of what I guess is glacial silt picked up from the river bars. Within a few hours of the wind change the brilliant green sphagnum moss carpeting the spruce forest was covered with a layer of rather drab beige.

   The dust and the cold have continued unabated for three days. This morning I noticed the river was beginning to freeze. Each channel had about a foot or two of ice lining the shore. Like breakup in the spring, the river is carrying chunks of ice downstream, ice that has apparently been ripped from the shoreline in the narrow canyons back in the mountains.

Day 12, September 26 (Low 18, High 32, light snow)
   The cold continues, the work on the roof still on hold. I packed moss around the base of the cabin, and with the first big snow I will shovel snow against the cabin walls up to the windows for insulation.

   The big eddy is frozen over, but the main channels are still running free. I don't think the cold will last, but who knows?

Day 13, September 27 (Low 29, High 35, clear)
   Squirrels. Red squirrels. The cabin sits right in a grove of spruce trees, the arboreal home of a dozen or more red squirrels. Actually, like foreigners and other strangers they all look alike to me so I don't know how many there are. For the past six years the cabin has been home for some of them, as evidenced by the nests I had to clean out on my arrival.

The squirrels still hold a proprietary interest in my new home, as shown by their scampering over the roof and through the attached workshed, which is not chinked so well as the cabin proper. I am scolded vociferously whenever I show myself outside. I have had to bring all the large scraps of foam rubber in from the workshed because I may need some later, and it began to disappear with alarming rapidity during a spate of nest building about a week ago. That activity seems to have abated to be replaced by the rather frantic-looking process of collecting and storing spruce cones, probably inspired by the current chilly weather.

I should not dwell too much on this relatively mild weather since in a month or two it will probably be a good seventy or eighty degrees colder, but at present, as warmly cold as it is, it is stopping me from work I must finish, and represents, in my mind, at least, the harbinger of winter.

So far, other than the three caribou, the squirrels have been the only constant sign of life around here. Minor exceptions: one fish, one spruce grouse, four waterfowl, a small flock of birds.

Day 14, September 28 (Low 32, High 32, light snow)

I'm beginning to wonder whether the roof will ever be completed. Is winter here? Actually it's no big problem. I'm doing the whole roof with one big double sheet of Visqueen, even though I'm doing a bit at a time. If I have to stop permanently before I finish, all the sod will be in place, although the new Visqueen will not be *under* some of it; it will be *over* it. That's all right. I think the integrity of the cabin will be OK, and I'll finish the job in the spring.

In the meantime I'm keeping busy with odd jobs like sewing the last of the missing (or, about-to-be-missing) buttons on clothing, and experimenting with my mobile oven. Today was cornbread time and it came out very well. Linguists will be pleased to note that here the bread does not, when it is finished baking, "come hot from the oven"; rather, the oven "comes hot from the bread."

Day 15, September 29 (Low 28, High 32, light snow)

I have just about exhausted all the easy-to-get, down-and-dead spruce. Later, when the river is frozen, I'll have access to whatever is on the other side, but not now. I have, however, been keeping my eye on a rather large island-cum-river bar near the cabin. It has been separated from me by a small but fast-flowing channel, but appears to have a good quantity of dry driftwood on it. After four or five days of subfreezing temperatures, ice has been bridging out from both sides but has not yet met in the middle.

I decided to help the bridging process out. I took the food cache ladder, which is about twenty feet long, and laid it over the still unfrozen channel. It required a certain amount of acrobatics, but within an hour I had cut and hauled to the cabin in six-foot lengths what should turn out to be at least a week's worth of fuel when split.

Also, I discovered two large spruce trees that had washed up and lodged on the island. For the Arctic, they are pretty good-sized — about two feet at the butt — and if the wood is good, could provide a cord or more.

This afternoon it began snowing, and by nightfall four or five inches were on the ground.

Day 16, September 30 (Low 32, High 45, cloudy)

It is a good thing I got wood from the island yesterday because today everything has changed. The snow vanished overnight; most of the ice is gone; and the river is up and rising. I heard the river before I saw it, and by its change of tone knew something was different. At a guess it appeared to have risen five or six inches during the night, probably from the ice and snow melting upstream as well as here.

The canoe had been on a gravel bar near the cabin since my arrival, but now that bar was almost under water, so I horsed the canoe up a steep embankment, thanks to Leonardo da Vinci, or whoever it was who first came across the concept of leverage. If you tie a length of rope to a substantially rooted tree and tie the other end as taut as you can get it to a canoe, and then put your weight on the middle of the intervening span, either the tree is going to move toward the canoe or vice versa. With admittedly somewhat limited experience in this rather arcane field of endeavor, I would nevertheless tend to favor the mobility of the canoe. It took a little while but eventually I tethered the canoe to a tree high enough so, if need be, it can remain there for the winter.

Later, when I checked the roof sod, it had thawed enough to be malleable, and I finally was able to work on the roof again. First I created a seal around the chimney, a job that had also had to wait for warmer weather. Then I attacked the roof, albeit somewhat maniacally, and had it two-thirds finished by nightfall.

Nightfall, by the way, is falling faster. When I arrived on September 15, there were about thirteen hours of possible sun-light; this according to the weather reports I hear from KOTZ, the AM radio station in Kotzebue, a little less north than I am but fairly close in latitude. But we are losing seven to eight minutes of daylight each day and it is now down to eleven hours and going quickly.

October

Day 17, October 1 (Low 32, High 32, snowing)
The weather is idiosyncratic if that word can be used in a meteorological context. The cold has returned, the sod froze overnight, and it snowed all day, so now there is another three or four inches on the ground; the river has stopped rising and is beginning to freeze again, and I am dead in the water as far as the roof is concerned. In response, I sublimated and baked chocolate chip cookies.

Day 18, October 2 (Low 30, High 32, cloudy)
Yesterday's snow was a little damp so it stuck wherever it landed. Every little tree branch, every twig has its touch of snow. The trees are thick around the cabin so the view in any direction is one of sculptured whiteness. The snow sucks sound right out of the air. It is very quiet. What will it be like when the river freezes, the wind ceases, and there is no sound at all? Then I will provoke the red squirrels to solicit their scolds.

I finished reading Robert Louis Stevenson's *Kidnapped* today. I believe I last read it when I was in my teens. What made it fascinating, reading this particular author at this time here in the Arctic, was the fact that only last winter I had climbed a hill in Western Samoa to visit his tomb, a truly magic spot overlooking the capital, Apia, and the reef guarding the harbor. I seem to be involved in contrasts lately. To wit, in recent years: winters in the Sonoran Desert and the Grand Canyon, the Himalayas of Nepal, the Alaska Range, the South Pacific, alternating with summers in Denali National Park, Alaska. And now, an Arctic winter and presumably another summer in Denali.

Reading R.L.S. reminded me again that as accurate historians we humanoids don't do very well. For the past decade or so the hippies and the flower children of the 1960s have been heaped with scorn by the caretakers of the English language for introducing the improper usage of the word *like*. "Like man, that was far out!" Or, "He like took a tab of acid and split." From page 242 of *Kidnapped* written in 1886 comes the following: " *'What's like wrong with him?' she said at last."*

Day 19, October 3 (Low 30, High 33, cloudy)

Since the weather was not too splendid I decided to work indoors this morning. With the aid of a flashlight — there is not a hell of a lot of light in here even in broad daylight with three kerosene lanterns going — which makes me wonder what it will be like this winter in narrow daylight. Become one with the mole, I guess.

Anyway, with the aid of a flashlight I explored every nook and cranny of the area where the walls meet the floor and administered a dose of moss where it appeared to be needed. The outer walls are still in abeyance as regards chinking. Once the roof is finished, about all that remains to be done to be completely winterized is to staple a layer of clear plastic Mylar over the windows, which will leave an air pocket for insulation — a sort of instant Thermopane.

Speaking of the roof — writing and speaking are essentially the same if there is no one to listen and no one to read — I attempted to work on it even though the temperature was right at freezing. I was able to complete about a four-by-eight-foot piece before my work gloves froze and my fingers would no longer bend. If I can get about three hours of above forty degrees I can finish the bloody thing.

I found some old tattered rubber boots in a corner of the workshed. Based on this discovery, tomorrow I'm going to wade over to the island I bridged to (laddered to?) a couple of days ago and try to find more wood. I'm down to only three or four days' supply.

Further experimenting and investigating into the arcane art of extemporaneous baking: Using the standard baking powder biscuit recipe, I cut it to one-third and made three pancake-shaped objects. These I tossed onto a hot griddle for about ten minutes. Ended up with a mutant. Tastes like a biscuit. Looks like a potato pancake. They were only about a half-inch thick, so instead of cutting them open I slapped butter and jam on one side and ate them like toast. Good.

Day 20, October 4 (Low 30, High 34, cloudy with light snow)

I donned my newfound rubber boots this morning and crossed the small channel without getting my feet soaked. There was about three inches of day-old snow and before I had gone far I could see that I had visitors last night. Wolves. Apparently three of them had crossed the river from the western side. When they neared my cabin two of the wolves stayed down near the river while the third made a close circuit around the cabin and then rejoined its companions and they proceeded downriver. I saw no sign of urine around the cabin except for my own, so I assume the cabin and its environs are still mine.

Late this afternoon the wind began to blow upriver, the light, occasional snow turned to rain, and the temperature climbed above freezing. I would wager that this will be another night when the snow will be gone by morning and the river once again on the rise. I'm beginning to find a direct correlation between rain and a feeling of depression. Having lived for a number of years in western Washington, where it *seems* to rain *all* the time, I find this phenomenon rather curious. Perhaps it is just age, linked in some way to the same compulsion that drives people lemminglike in winter from the northern states to the desert trailer courts of Arizona. Along with many other questions, maybe I can find an answer to that this winter.

Day 21, October 5 (Low 28, High 32, snow)

Most of the snow did vanish overnight, which doesn't make me a meteorological savant exactly, but its nice to be able to predict *something* once in awhile. This morning it began snowing again, and by noon there were about four inches on the ground and getting deeper.

When I attended the University of Washington, purely by chance I roomed or shared a house with one or more electrical engineering majors for much of the four years I was there. They were involved in a very narrow discipline. The only brush they had with the humanities, which for them included everything *not* in double E, was one survey course called Humanities 101, or something like that. It attempted to teach them everything they should know about poetry, literature, sociology, psychology, history, music, etcetera, etcetera, in one five-hour course. And that, boys and girls, is why most engineers are such jerks.

But I digress. I wish I had listened more carefully to some of the problems they had to solve. Because I have an electronic mystery and have been trying to solve it since I arrived here. Some background: For the past three years I have been trying to bring in the FM signal for KUAC in Fairbanks, a station at the University of Alaska which carries National Public Radio. This has taken place while I lived at Carlo Creek, about fifteen miles south of Denali. But even with the help of my friend Dan Rosenberg, who threw himself bodily into the endeavor and sent me special antennas from Seattle and San Francisco, it was to no avail.

So, I came to the cabin without any idea my luck would change. But, Eureka! The nearest station, KOTZ from Kotzebue, carries many of the programs from NPR including "All Things Considered," the best radio news show in the history of mankind, as well as a lot of jazz and classical music. And it comes in loud and clear.

And I came loaded for bear, radiowise: One radio, two large twelve-volt fence batteries, two transformers to change the voltage from twelve to six, a dozen C batteries which is what my radio normally is powered by, and two dozen D batteries, the latter intended for flashlights. Alas, the fence batteries (one was supposed to last for the whole winter) do not work. Or, the transformers don't work. I can't tell which because I don't have a tool for determining current flow.

It's difficult to believe that I purchased one dead fence battery, let alone two, but I suppose it is possible. It's also possible that both transformers are kaput, but not likely. In the meantime, this morning I built a makeshift frame to hold four D batteries, which add up to six volts the same as four C's. By juggling D's and C's I should have a couple of months of radio time. On the other hand, maybe six or seven months of silence, besides what exists in nature, would be beneficial.

Dusk. The snow is now almost seven inches deep. The river is freezing. Little cumulus clouds of ice, like puffs of cotton under water, are starting to gather in the big eddy. They jam up in the narrow channels before eventually breaking through. In the big eddy they drift around and around counterclockwise, like slow dancers in a ballroom. The snow is moist and sticks where it alights. Looking north from where the river is bringing its ice, mountains, trees and the river bars are a uniform white. There is only the river for contrast.

Day 22, October 6 (Low 28, High 32, clear)

Almost a foot of snow on the ground this morning! Very quiet, and very beautiful. It was probably premature but in honor of the occasion I spent a couple of hours shoveling snow up against the outside walls for insulation. This snow will probably melt and I will have to do it over again, but it was worth the effort just to see the visual effect. With the roof covered with snow, and the sides banked up to the bottom of the windows, the cabin is nearly invisible. Like the Cheshire cat, there is nothing left but the smile.

The sun came out for awhile today and the scenery was glorious. North, the Brooks Range looked as if it had got a lot of snow over the past week. According to the radio, Kotzebue is flooding and things are blowing away in Bethel. My valley, on the other hand, is feeling snug.

Last night I was visited for the first time (the first that I was aware of, anyway) by one of the members of the bottom of the food chain. It was either a lemming, vole or shrew, I don't know which. I would like to share, but from what I've heard, they tend to want it all. So far it's been too fast for me to catch. During the night I could hear it chewing, through what I suspected was Reynolds Wrap covering a newly baked pie. But this morning the only damage I could find was a few nibbles on a quarter pound of margarine. Doing battle with these creatures, *mano-a-mano*, as it were—may prove to be an interesting if not frustrating divertissement through the long winter nights.

The trees outside are so loaded with snow that a puff of breeze or a fast-traveling squirrel can trigger an arboreal avalanche starting at the top and building on the way down. When it hits the ground it sounds like a herd of caribou galloping by the cabin, whump! whump! whump!

Tonight the unknown member of the bottom of the food chain returned. (Hereafter referred to as the Unknown M.B.F.C., deceased.) The Unknown M.B.F.C. deceased had been warned. I have it in writing only about three paragraphs back. So when he returned I rendered him *hors de combat* with a brilliantly executed combination parry and thrust with a kindling stick, and then gave him a Viking funeral in the stove.

Day 23, October 7 (Low 26, High 28, cloudy)

Nothing is happening today. There is a kind of stasis. It's not snowing and it's not melting. The river is not freezing, nor are the edges thawing. The big eddy is half ice and half water. There is a little wind, but not much. I cut some wood today and that's about it. In fact, the day was so blah I cooked macaroni and cheese for dinner. And so ends Day 23 with neither a bang nor a whimper.

Well . . . not quite. About an hour after dark, around seven, Mike and a female companion showed up. I hadn't even heard the sound of his outboard. So much for being alert to sounds in the wilderness. Mike had to come up to get some supplies and a larger chain saw. He will leave me a small chain saw, which at this point I can use because the tree I was cutting on today is really too thick for my bow saw. Susan just came up for the ride and to stay at Mike's cabin for a few days.

Mike will go back to his fish camp tomorrow and probably won't be back until mid-November because fishing has been poor. The fish are intended for dog food, and without it, it's not likely he could afford a dog team. In the meantime Mike said that 1) If the moss is solid in the chinks, it's OK; and 2) He thinks the stove, with my repairs, will last the winter. So, other than finishing the roof, gathering wood and fetching water, I am semiretired, and free to belly up to my typewriter when the muse is ready.

Day 24, October 8 (Low 29, High 30, cloudy)

I helped Mike off-load several bags of commercial dog food from his canoe. His dogs are now at fish camp but up until now he hasn't had a sled there. I went over to his place wearing snowshoes to tramp down the trail so he and Susan could push and pull a sled which he took with him when he left at about three.

On departing Mike left me a chain saw, gas and oil, and a saw sharpener. He also left me some rubber waders, Blazo for my Coleman lantern, four whitefish and one char, frozen but ungutted. I chopped a little wood that turned out to be rather moist, which meant that I spent the rest of the day playing with the fire. Tonight I will take the bath that was interrupted last night, an activity that, if my olfactory senses are no better than my hearing, is sorely needed.

Day 25, October 9 (Low 26, High 32, cloudy)

I put Mike's waders on this morning and blazed through six inches of water with a four-foot margin of safety. I carried three logs across the small channel and called it a day as far as wood was concerned. Also, I convinced myself that roof work is finished until spring, so I tidied up and stapled down the Visqueen. It can go the winter as is, or if it becomes tropical I'll finish it. I made a batch of chocolate chip cookies and read for the rest of the day. In the afternoon a gray jay came by, but he didn't stay around long. Perhaps I should put out some bird feed and gain some company.

Day 26 October 10 (Low 28, High 32, partly cloudy)

Today is Columbus Day and according to what I hear on KOTZ in Kotzebue, it is being celebrated there. Why? Most Kotze-buebians are Eskimo. The day Mr. Columbus set foot on North American soil was the day that signaled the beginning of the end of Eskimo culture, and all Native culture in the New World. They shouldn't celebrate — they should go out and spear an Italian.

Today, with my post-industrial-revolution chain saw, I cut as much wood as I have in the past three weeks with the bow saw. There is a negative lesson there. I'm saving sweat and polluting the environment with noise and fumes. I'm going to butcher one more dead tree and put the damn chain saw away.

Big Jim Watt resigned as Secretary of Interior yesterday. Maybe that's what the Eskimos are celebrating in Kotzebue. If it isn't, it should be, and I'll join 'em.

Day 27, October 11 (Low 28, High 33, clear)

A mystery. I had three down trees located on the island in front of the cabin. I cut one up yesterday, dug the second one out of foot-deep snow, and the third tree is flat lost. I thought I remembered exactly where it was located but after a half-hour of probing in the snow it was not to be found. From now on I'll flag a tree that I'm not going to cut right away. I spent the bulk of a very sunny day shoveling snow around the wood-chopping and storage area, and around the outdoor privy so, unlike the missing tree, these two areas will not become "lost" during the next snowstorm.

Susan brought over a hunk of caribou this evening and I whipped up a repast of boo garlic steak, dehydrated potatoes, and alfalfa sprout salad. She is going downriver on the morrow.

Shortly after dinner a marten began prowling around the cabin, drawn I suspect by the smell of caribou meat hanging in the storm porch. I opened the door and stepped outside thinking it would run off, but it didn't, at least not right away. It was completely unafraid. It stood there about ten feet away looking directly at me for what seemed like a minute, then turned and bounded gracefully away across the snow. Beautiful brown fur, wide open face, bushy tail. I could have shot it easily, but had no reason to. I have heard stories that even food caches are not proof against them, so we will see. (Something chewed on the cabin roof most of the night, but I think it was squirrel, not marten.)

Day 28, October 12 (Low 26, High 32, cloudy)

Susan did not leave as planned, so we shared another meal. Prepackaged beef stroganoff (at least six years old, left behind in the food cache), sprouts, dehydrated string beans, and baking powder biscuits with honey.

I chopped, hauled and sawed wood all day. I had to ford the same stream twice which meant loading the sled, off-loading and carrying across the stream, on-loading, hauling, off-loading and carrying across the stream, on-loading and hauling. At one point I stopped in mid-haul and queried myself out loud: "Why am I doing this?" After some thought I decided there was embodied in that query two questions and two answers. If "doing this" means why am I spending the winter above the Arctic Circle, the answer is so frought with metaphysical implications that I would just say, "Who knows, and who cares." On the other hand, if "doing this" means the activity of cutting and hauling wood, the answer is easy. It's to stay alive. A worthy motive if there ever was one.

Having arrived at that point in a rather brief Q&A session, I decided to continue cutting and hauling.

Day 29, October 13 (Low 28, High 32, cloudy)
Susan apparently left early this morning. I found a note saying goodbye and happy winter. It was stuck in a snowbank outside. As usual I chopped wood. Big day for baking! Lemon pie and peanut butter cookies.
Medical bulletin: I have either got a stiff neck, or sore glands in the neck. I can't tell which. Will watch it.

Day 30, October 14 (Low 28, High 32, cloudy)
Laundry. Wood. Third game of the World Series. Whitefish dinner.

Day 31, October 15 (Low 16, High 22, clear)
One month on the river! Flime ties!
From my river viewpoint I could see two sets of tracks this morning. They are across the river so I couldn't check them up close. Suffice it for now to note that they were made by either caribou, moose, bear or wolves.

Day 32, October 16 (Low 10, High 20, clear)
It's getting cold around here. Yesterday and today were beautiful, sunny, clear and cold. The river is again carrying a lot of ice. Freeze-up may be just around the time corner.
I entertained a fit of stubbornness yesterday and decided to continue the search for the tree that vanished during the last big snow. I found it after much probing, and today cut it up and stacked it in my growing wood yard.
Last night I went to bed with a stiff neck and a headache for the second night in a row. Not having immediate access to the National Center For the Prevention of Disease, or its equivalent, I began to conduct my own investigation of this local version of Legionnaires' disease. In perusing my copy of *The Complete Medical Guide*, in the section on poisons, I began to see a slim possibility that this cabin may be so well insulated that I'm breathing little else but kerosene fumes each evening. So tonight I have opened an air vent (which I had previously sealed for the

winter) and am not using the Aladdin lamp, which tends to burn a lot of kerosene.

More visitors this evening. (This place is getting a lot of traffic lately.) Christy and Doug Carnes, a couple who live downriver about fifteen miles near Mike's fish camp, hiked up to get chain-saw parts from Mike's cabin. They are going to set up an Alaska chain-sawmill and cut some planks. They live in a sod igloo with their three-year-old daughter, Anna, who is being baby-sat by Susan. Tomorrow they will take the canoe down. I wish I had known their plans, because yesterday I spent an inordinate amount of energy moving the canoe still farther above the river.

Familiarity may breed contempt, as the saying goes, but it also breeds familiarity. What started out in my mind as members of the bottom of the food chain, I now think of as simply B.F.C.'s. Another B.F.C. came around last night, but did not leave, corporally at any rate. Along with my rule about never smiling at a gorilla, you can add (if you are a B.F.C.) the admonition: Never jump into the bottom of an empty cornflakes box.

Day 33, October 17 (Low 5, High 15, clear and sunny)

"Dear Mrs. B.F.C., I regret to inform you that your son was killed in action on this date. You will be proud to learn that he gave his life in a rear-guard skirmish in the kindling box. His bravery undoubtedly was responsible for the safe return of the remaining members of his patrol. It is believed his demise was eventuated by an aging member of the home guard, the young of the enemy having been sent to the war in Lebanon.

"Do not ask for whom the bell tolls; It does not toll for thee. It tolls for the unknown members of the B.F.C."

Doug and Christy left this morning. They popped the canoe in between two fast-moving chunks of ice and tooled on downriver as if they were going for a Sunday picnic on the Thames. The temperature was about five degrees above zero. So, I am now left with my feet as the sole means of locomotion out of here.

I discovered another down tree today! I had noticed a big tangle of stump upriver but for some reason didn't associate it with the idea that there might be a tree attached to it. Today I went up to cut off some of the roots and discovered there was more than met the eye. I'll dig out the snow tomorrow and do some cutting on it.

Possible sunlight is now down to nine hours, according to the radio, but here, because of the mountains lying to the east and west, the sun is visible only from ten in the morning to three in the afternoon, or about five hours of potential direct sunlight.

I ran across more wolf tracks on the way back from the newfound tree, but they were two or three days old.

Day 34, October 18 (Low -5*, High 10, clear and sunny)
*First below zero!

I hauled the chain saw all the way out to the newfound tree, only to discover it wouldn't start in the near-zero temperature. Had it been mine I would have thrown it into the river. So I wasted half a day trying to cut an oversized log with a bow saw. On the other hand, I have a lot of days remaining to "waste" so why should I complain? There is an old seven-foot-long bucksaw crouched in the corner of the work shed which I shall attempt to resurrect tomorrow. If my arm hasn't atrophied in this high tech society of ours, the bow saw and bucksaw will start every time.

Day 35, October 19 (Low -15, High 5, sunny)

Too cold to get wood today. I started out but found I was walking into a north wind of twenty to thirty mph, which made for a rather frigid chill factor, so I turned back and baked a loaf of honey walnut bread (from a recipe in *The Tassajara Bread Book*). There are too many options here — a body could go crazy just trying to figure out what to do next.

What I did next, after the bread, was to construct a B.F.C. trap from an eagle kerosene lamp chimney, three pieces of wood, a sheet of Reynolds Wrap, and a small wedge of Gruyere cheese. This latter activity seemed to be required by the continuing nocturnal visitations by members of that group.

Day 36, October 20 (Low -20, High -5, sunny)

It was cold today but not windy, so I was able to venture forth for wood. The snow is now frozen and packed so hard the snowshoes are no longer needed. The big bucksaw worked fine, but not in confined quarters, which necessitated prior excavation of a good deal of snow. The saw is really designed for two-man work, but I discovered I could handle it, and it does start well even at subzero temperatures. While I was sawing, a red fox came by, about one hundred yards away across the river. It was really curious about me. Several times it started on its way only to stop and watch as I renewed sawing. It had the reddish brown color phase. I imagined it was in search of B.F.C.s. Had we been able to communicate I could have touted it onto a dandy location — my cabin.

I made winter official today by covering the windows with the clear plastic Mylar I had brought from Fairbanks. I did it not so much to keep out the cold — it's already pretty cozy — but to stop the ice from collecting on the inside of the glass, which blocks a lot of light.

Day 37, October 21 (Low -15, High 0, sunny)

Nothing. Today I did nothing. I saw nothing, felt nothing. I hardly left the cabin. I need a project. I have a project. It's personified by that little black case sitting over in the corner. It contains a machine for writing. I'm avoiding it. The winter I spent at Carlo Creek in the Alaska Range, I stared at that little black case until mid-January, when I finally opened it and began rewriting the Nepal story, *Getting High In the Himalayas*. This year I *will* begin writing *something* by November first, or consign the damn machine to the river and quit playing these mind games.

Errant thought with regard to typewriters and a few other items such as Ping-Pong paddles. I must be an audiophile, because I can't type with anything but a manual typewriter. (The only thing possible here.) But in more civilized climes, electric typewriters, not to mention word processors, just don't sound right to me, and for the life of me I can't use 'em. Same for Ping-Pong paddles. I'm a pretty good journeyman player with sandpaper-covered paddles, but can't do diddly with those effete soft rubber paddles. They just don't *sound* right.)

Last night I toyed with the idea of making a major commitment to join the battle of saving the wolf. I don't at this point know what I could or would do, but it seems like a project I could sink my teeth into, no pun intended. Maybe a book. I'll let the idea simmer.

Day 38, October 22 (Low -15, High 0, sunny)

I'm not certain I can describe accurately what happened earlier

today, but I will try. It is now about four hours after the incident.

In midafternoon, since it was sunny and windless I decided to go out to the tree I had found earlier and do a little sawing. The temperature was right at zero. I did not take my rifle. This was the same tree I had been sawing on previously during the red fox encounter. It's located about a half-mile north of the cabin. I had been there only a few minutes, clearing snow away from the tree, and was looking down at the place where I intended to start my cut, when something at the farthest extent of my peripheral vision attracted my attention. It's a little difficult to describe. I was looking down near my feet but what I saw was movement several hundred yards upstream and across the river. (This is something I have apparently learned since becoming a wilderness tour guide — "seeing" the big picture while focusing on a much more narrow field of view.) Once I looked in that direction I knew, without even a shade of doubt, and without thinking, it was a grizzly. It was still a long way off, and on the other side of an ice-choked, fast-flowing river, but it was coming in my direction. I didn't hesitate. I left the bucksaw and shovel right where they were, picked up the Hudson's Bay ax and sled, and began walking toward the cabin. The bear neither saw nor smelled me, but it kept on coming.

As I walked, I periodically checked the bear's progress. Each time I looked he was still four or five hundred yards away, still on the other side of the river, and still unaware of my presence. When I reached the trees near my cabin—I had been on an open river bar, as was the bear — I ran to the cabin, grabbed my .30-30 rifle, and ran back out to the viewpoint in front of the cabin.

The bear was still approaching, much nearer now. As he drew closer he began pausing and sniffing the air. I don't think he could smell me, but probably could smell the smoke from the fire in the cabin. I was hoping the bear, like the red fox, would continue down *his* side of the river, and that would be that: My first grizzly sighting in the Arctic. That wasn't to be. When the bear was still about one hundred yards upstream he turned and headed purposefully for the river. I have watched too many grizzlies at Denali National Park not to know the bear was about to come over to my side of the river. In retrospect I think I should have fired a warning shot then. The noise of the rifle plus whatever small difficulty the icy river represented might have dissuaded him, but I didn't. The bear walked out on the icy shelf, hesitated a moment, then plunged into the torrent of ice and water.

He was across in seconds. Water and ice flew in all directions as he shook himself, and at that moment I put a bullet into the snow a few feet in front of him. The sound was tremendous, echoing off the water and back from the trees and nearby hills. The grizzly raised up as if to stand on his hind legs, went back down on all fours, moved his head from side to side, and began walking — not directly toward me and the cabin, because he was faced with an abrupt little cliff in that direction. He was heading toward the low spot I had used moments ago in coming back from the tree. I put two more bullets in front of him, and then showed myself for the first time, yelling and waving, knowing that the normal reaction of most grizzlies to human encounters is to avoid them. Not this one. He stopped momentarily after each shot, looked in my direction when I yelled, but kept coming. At that point he was about seventy-five yards upstream and about thirty feet below me.

Things now became rather surrealistic. (This has happened to me before, most notably when I made my first parachute jump. There were two of me, the person performing the action and a second person, a sort of disassociated spectator.) I had a strong feeling of inevitability. I *knew* the bear was heading for my cabin even though I had now lost sight of him; he was hidden by a jutting little promontory and the spruce trees surrounding the cabin. I can't say why — he could have followed the trail to Mike's cabin, or turned and gone upriver — but I was certain he was heading my way. I sprinted for the cabin, only fifty feet away.

I ran into the storm porch, closed and bolted the door, and wedged a good-sized spruce pole against the middle of the door. The latter was something I had learned in New York City, of all places. (The only way a door like that can be opened is to knock it off its hinges or shatter it, which I later decided a grizzly could probably do quite easily.) I did the same thing to the inner door. I was sure I didn't have much time, so I replaced the three shells I had fired, and looked around for something to make noise with. I grabbed a large metal pot and a hatchet, hoping I could scare the bear away with noise. Then I waited.

This all took place in only a minute or two, when suddenly the front window was completely filled with the image of a huge grizzly bear. There were no windows facing north, the direction from which the bear was coming, so its appearance was both instantaneous and appalling. This is a small cabin, partially sunk in the ground, and the windows are not very high above ground level. By piling snow on the lower walls I had in effect put the windows at ground level. Now, an adult grizzly bear and I were face to face, about five feet apart, separated by a few thin panes of glass.

I began banging the hatchet against the pot. From inside the cabin the noise was horrendous but, I later decided, probably not outside. The grizzly took a step toward the window and almost casually, it seemed, smashed the window with one brief swipe of his right front paw. Then, in retrospect it was in slow motion, he put both paws on the sill and with pieces of broken glass still clattering to the floor, stuck his enormous head through the shattered window. I had already dropped the hatchet and pot. I picked up my rifle, which was loaded and cocked, aimed between the eyes, which was no big deal since the end of the rifle barrel was a scant two feet from his head, and fired.

The bear was knocked back out of the window by the bullet's impact. He fell on his side and without the slightest twitch or spasm was still. Blood began flowing from his nostrils and mouth. I stuck the barrel of the rifle out the broken window and fired another shot behind the ear.

Then I leaned the rifle against the bed and began talking to the grizzly. I do not have particularly outstanding reflexes, either mental or physical. I was well aware of that when I came up here, so I had to decide in advance what I would do if I encountered a bear. What I decided was to avoid any encounter away from the cabin if at all possible. This mostly just requires a little common sense and alertness. But, what about *at* the cabin? I had decided that a bear prowling in the vicinity of the cabin had, of course, to be watched carefully, but that only if it attempted to break in would it have to be shot.

For the first few minutes after the killing the one overpowering thought in my mind was not about fixing the window, even though in the subzero temperature the cabin was already getting cold. Nor was it the removal of the carcass. It was somehow to communicate to the bear, and receive some sort of exculpation from the bear. I suppose I was more than a little hysterical at that point, but to the other observer, the other me, it seemed perfectly natural to explain this to the grizzly.

I do not now feel proud about its death. There is no sense of macho accomplishment. I eventually went outside and bled it, and moved it a little way from the door. It was too heavy to move far, and I could not dismember it so soon. Maybe tomorrow, if the wolves, or another bear — God forbid — don't get it tonight. Another bear would sit on and eat it for several days, and I would probably be forced to kill it too, just so I could get outside to get wood and water.

Day 39, October 23 (Low -5, High 5, cloudy)

I have re-read what I wrote last night, and it does seem a little hysterical, but it conveys in a general way how I was feeling. In self defense I should mention that post-hysteria is better than pre-; the latter can get you into trouble.

I slept little last night. I kept getting up and shining a flashlight on the bear, hoping, I guess, that it would somehow just vanish. I had cut its throat about a half-hour after I'd shot it. Before I had done that I had repaired the window with clear plastic, which in retrospect seems like an odd choice of priorities.

I think it will be some time before I can confront exactly what this incident means. I do have the feeling that this was in some way predestined, and that in this encounter I in some way failed my responsibility. What would have happened if I had not fired that final shot when I did? It was the purposefulness displayed by the bear from the very beginning, how he reacted to my warning shots on the riverbed and, ultimately, how he responded to my pounding on the kettle that contributed to the feeling of inevitability I referred to earlier.

On the other hand, the grizzly was not acting in what would normally be considered an aggressive manner. He was not growling; no false charges; in fact, no aggressive displays at all, except for his determination to check out the cabin.

The bear did break the window, but almost casually as I have noted. This cabin is quite soundproof, and what sounded to me like an Arctic version of Times Square at midnight on New Year's

Eve, may have been loud enough outside only to arouse the bear's curiosity. I will never know, and not knowing, will always wonder whether the bear was preparing to charge or retreat at the moment I fired.

There is some small evidence for the latter. It now appears that although I aimed between the eyes, the bullet apparently entered through the mouth or throat and probably lodged in the brain. The bear is more likely to have raised his head if he intended to back out, but I suppose that is debatable. What is not arguable is that if the grizzly was going to charge into the cabin and I had not fired, I would not be writing this. (Today I strung two quarter-inch steel cables across the window in question, which won't stop a bear, but will slow him down.)

A question I do not like to ask is, what if I had not gone to get wood and had not seen the bear when he was still a long way off? I could have been bathing, washing dishes, etcetera, and the rifle could have been hanging in its usual place on the wall near the bed. Or, what if I had been out at the woodpile when the bear showed up, cut off from the cabin and my rifle?

I spent most of the daylight hours today skinning and butchering the bear. I didn't do a very good job, but I did get it finished. I stored the pelt, head, fore and hind legs up in the food cache. I rolled the remainder, still very heavy, onto a sled and dragged it several hundred feet away from the cabin. After wrapping it in two large plastic garbage bags and pouring water on it in an attempt to seal it in ice, I covered it with a large mound of snow, and then covered that with small logs and tree branches. With a little more snow and continued cold it should be safe from other animals. I have no desire for the meat, but Mike may be able to use it for feeding his sled dogs. If not, at least it's no longer right in front of the cabin door.

Day 40, October 24 (Low -15, High 0, some sun)

Delayed reaction to the bear incident. It has really colored my feeling about this place. If it wasn't a forty-five-mile hike out, I would probably have left today, the way I was feeling. Maybe it will go away.

Also, having had a chance to think a little more clearly about this whole incident, and the grizzly itself, I've come to the conclusion that there is really no logical reason for a bear to be out roaming around this late in the season. It's been very cold for some time, and the snow covers any vegetation the bear might normally eat, although it may have had a chance for a late kill of moose or caribou. Still, I think it is just too late in the year, especially here in the Arctic, for bears to be out of their dens. Maybe the bear failed to get the proper signals telling it when to prepare its den; maybe the den collapsed; maybe the bear was diseased. Something was out of whack.

Day 41, October 25 (Low -15, High -2, sunny)

Less than eight hours a day of sunlight beginning tomorrow and counting down.

As with the pilot who crashes a plane and lives, it's important to fly again soon or it may not happen at all. That is sort of what I had to do today. I had to bite the metaphorical bullet and return to the wood tree from where I had first seen the bear. I had avoided this trip two days ago with the rationalization that I had to skin and butcher the remains. Yesterday I had no such excuse, but I didn't go even though I had planned to. Why? Well, because I had this terrible advance feeling of *deja vu* — that I would spot another bear, try unsuccessfully to frighten it off, and end up killing yet another grizzly.

I felt so strongly that this would happen that I very nearly did not go again today. But even worse was this feeling of paralysis I've been going through. Psychologically, this cabin and this area are no longer my turf. I couldn't enjoy it without peering behind each tree, and looking over my shoulder as I moved around, even inside the cabin with the door bolted.

So I said to hell with it, grabbed my rifle and sled, and went out to get some wood. Nothing happened, needless to say, but I spent far more time looking around than I did sawing — no doubt a wise precaution, but I felt it to be a negative personal reaction. It boils down to this: If I must go around trailing trepidation as I have the past couple of days, this true wilderness experience is being corrupted, either by me or by circumstance. The results are the same. If this feeling continues I have two choices, it seems to me. I must leave or I must put the gun away and deal with the grizzly on some other level. I don't want to die, but I don't want to kill another bear, either. Which probably means, if this were a rational world, I will leave. We'll see.

Day 42, October 26 (Low -15, High -2, partly cloudy)
I broke into my two-week (estimated) wood reserve today, which means the river had better freeze over soon or I'm going to begin ranging far afield for fuel. There is still about one day's wood at the site where I have been cutting most recently, but that's it for the known wood supply. (I'm referring, of course, only to dead and down, or standing, dead spruce trees.) The river could freeze any day, but I think it would take forty below or more for a couple of days to do it. The channels have narrowed by more than half as the edges freeze and the volume of water decreases.

Two apparently military jets flew over very high today, coincidentally while I was listening on the shortwave radio to news of the Lebanon massacre and the U.S. invasion of Grenada. We are very close to the USSR here, and since these are the first military planes I have seen, I suspect there is a connection.

Speaking of connections, at the top of this page in the original journal is the word "retribalizing." I obviously put it there to remind myself of something I wanted to write about. I wish to hell I knew what it was!

Day 43, October 27 (Low -10, High 0, cloudy)
Baked my first Arctic apple pie today using freeze-dried apples. I haven't sampled it yet, but it looks pretty good. It took twice as long as normal to bake it, but that was because of wet wood. A curious phenomenon: With temperatures below zero for the past two weeks or so, all the wood I have stockpiled appears to be bone-dry when I split it and it splits just like cedar. But as soon as it gets inside the cabin, it's wet. Either there is moisture there to begin with, but being frozen it *feels* dry, or the wood attracts moisture from the cabin just as a magnet does metal filings. In any case, it's been difficult keeping a good, hot fire going lately.

I haven't had any headaches for quite awhile, which tells me that ventilating the cabin was the correct solution to that problem.

There is a can of foul-smelling kerosene out back. Mike said it was jet fuel left behind by a now-defunct mining outfit which had a chopper. The kerosene was "rescued" some time ago for what was then an unknown future use. A use, I now believe, whose time has come. The odor is very strong; so strong, in fact, that if used in a kerosene lantern, which I tried, it will run you right out of the cabin. So I poured a little of it along each outside windowsill and around the snow-covered bear carcass, in case another bear shows up. I figured it wouldn't smell too appetizing, and might even cover up other smells that would. I know a bear has an incredible sense of smell, but I don't know how discriminatory it is. This is a test of sorts.

Day 44, October 28 (Low -5, High 10, cloudy)

The temperature went up to ten above today and it actually felt warm!

I was downriver about half a mile cutting wood when I suddenly saw what I took at first to be a dozen or so caribou running in a line. It turned out to be a team of fourteen sled dogs with Mike riding on the rear of the sled. Mike had come up to get a bigger sled so he could ferry some cargo from the village to his cabin. He wants me to return with him to his fish camp for a Halloween celebration at the Igloo. I'll probably go — especially after he showed me where there was a good supply of dry wood downriver about a mile. It sounds like an easy decision, but the thought of being around a half-dozen people all of a sudden after the past month and a half is somewhat disquieting.

Day 45, October 29 (Low -5, High 10, partly cloudy)

I got some wood today and baked cookies to take downriver tomorrow for the Halloween party. Participants will be Doug, Christy, Susan, Mike and me, and, the reason for the party, Doug and Christy's daughter, Anna.

The river "bridged" over with ice yesterday in two places near the cabin, but I don't think it will be safe to cross for a few days yet. It began overflowing yesterday, and the river bars where I have been cutting wood for the past several weeks will soon be covered with ice. Overflow is a curious phenomenon, neither ice nor water, but something in between, a viscous, partly frozen mush that seeks its own level and spreads out, eventually covering the river from bank to bank. Mike says this has already happened throughout the lower segment of the river up to within two miles of here. We'll be taking the dogs (or rather, they will be taking us) down an inside trail tomorrow for the first six miles and then follow the river for the next nine miles.

With regard to the bear, Mike was suitably impressed as evidenced by his carrying his rifle between his cabin and mine, something he does not ordinarily do this time of the year. Mike said he would have shot to kill at the time I was firing warning shots. I do not know whether this makes me feel good or just stupid.

Day 46, October 30 (Low 5, High 10, light snow)

South in the taiga (spruce forest) by dog power. I am always amazed how these relatively small animals can work so long and hard, and so together. The word "dog team" is no misnomer. The trip down was beautiful, the first six miles through snow-covered spruce along a winding trail Mike had pioneered, cutting a right-of-way where the trees were too thick to penetrate. And then nine miles on some of the strangest river terrain I have ever seen. Big blocks of ice of startling blue, upthrust in odd conjunctions by the force of the river, hidden now below the layer of ice. The river was frozen over but still active with overflow, which we had to skirt. Small, statuelike projections called niggerheads (surely they will never be called black heads) also had to be avoided. Frozen slush covered with snow, softening the sharp angles, visually, but not in fact; dangerous to dogs because it can cut their paws, and dangerous to us because the uneven surface can flip over a sled. It happened to us, but only once. Unlike the Nenana River, which along the stretch where I had spent another winter simply froze over with some odd contours where summer rapids lurk, this one becomes an obstacle course to be negotiated with care.

We reached Doug and Christy's in midafternoon. They live in a sod igloo. (Build a frame and roof with wood; stack sod outside about a foot thick, and frame in windows and door; usually built into the side of a hill, as is Doug and Christy's. "Igloo" is the Eskimo word for "house," including the one made from snow we all grew up learning about, but also including a variety of other structures.)

We picked up Annathea, six-year-old daughter of Doug and Christy, and took her with us to Mike's fish camp where the three of us spent the night. We all slept in sleeping bags on caribou hides in Mike's wall tent. Wall tents are strange. As long as a fire is going in the stove it is warm and very comfortable, even with temperatures of twenty or thirty below, but once the fire is allowed to die there is nothing to retain the heat, and the temperature very quickly matches that of outside — in this case, about twenty below zero. The dogs slept outside, chained to stakes, curled up in the snow, occasionally providing us with an Arctic lullaby.

Day 47, October 31 (Low -15, High 0, cloudy)

All Hallows Eve, less popularly known as James Ramsey's natal eve. Halloween in the Arctic! You will tip no outdoor toilets here. Slit trenches are apparently *de riguer*. (At Mike's fish camp, we use half of a fifty-gallon drum and then burn it.)

We had dinner at Doug and Christy's — boo burgers, popcorn, pumpkin pie topped with Arctic ice cream (milk, oil, vanilla and snow and add whatever flavor you want). Good oh! We topped off the evening by taking turns reading aloud stories by Edgar Allen Poe. The celebrants were Doug, Christy, Anna, Susan, Mike and me. Anna had made me a birthday present, a little hand-crocheted chain made from red yarn.

I spent much of last night helping Anna with her first-grade correspondence studies. She is very bright, and because she is being tutored at home by her parents, is probably a couple of years ahead of her urban peers. Mike and I slept on the floor of their new sod igloo, not yet completed. Plenty of caribou hides, but still cold. The night was clear and starry.

November

Day 48, November 1 (Low 0, High 10, cloudy)

Today we loaded about a thousand pounds of frozen fish onto Mike's fish-camp food cache. It represents the catch for the season and not a very good one, according to Mike. He will take me back tomorrow, before heading downriver again to pick up supplies in the village. He should return in about two weeks. Today is my birthday, but no cause for celebration. After more than a half-century of these things, I consider them millstones, not milestones.

Day 49, November 2 (Low 0, High 5, clear)

Back upriver. On the return we stopped at Doug and Christy's, where I received, with much gratitude, a couple of pounds of ground boo burger, a half-dozen onions (FRESH!), a cabbage (ALSO!), and a handmade birthday card from Anna. The card depicted, among other things, a variety of suns; four yellow, one green, one blue and one red. I'll put it on the wall during the forthcoming dark ages to remind me of brighter times. Anna's name is a palindrome (reads and spells the same backward and forward) and in honor of this gift I shall *try* to compose a palindromic poem for her in time for Christmas.

On the way back Mike tied a gee pole to the front of the sled and a pair of short skis to the harness line. This setup is most often used by mushers when they have a heavily laden sled. Leverage by the person manning the gee pole helps the dogs turn the sled around sharp corners. Obviously we didn't need a gee pole operation since the only cargo at the time was me. I think Mike just wanted me to have the opportunity of riding the rear runners, operating the brake, and in general, fulfilling one of several thousand fantasies I am constantly juggling — this one entitled "Uklook of the Arctic." Mike rode the skis.

The dogs, eager to get home, were pulling flat out. I was standing on the rear runners trying not to fall off, while also trying to keep the sled upright. Mike, impossibly keeping his balance on the skis, pulled or pushed the gee pole avoiding a succession of trees by inches. All of this time he was riding, if that is the word, only inches in front of the sled. One misstep and he would have been behind us with sled-runner marks running the length of his body.

At one point Mike casually announced that we were soon going to encounter a little drop-off, and he would appreciate it if I would apply the brake so the sled would not land on him and the dogs when they hit bottom. At about the time I applied the foot brake, both Mike and the dogs disappeared over a small cliff. I, of course, followed shortly thereafter, believing in mid-plunge that both the sled and I were going to dig a very deep hole in the snow when we hit bottom. Not so. On impact the sled momentarily turned into a pretzel — like a raft in white water — before regaining its normal shape. Mike miraculously kept his footing on the skis — there are no foot straps nor fasteners — and the dogs never even broke stride. As for myself, having negotiated the chasm without falling off the sled or otherwise embarrassing myself in front of (actually behind) Mike and the dogs, I felt a little like Clark Kent as he exits a phone booth. I had instantaneously, so it seemed, been transformed into a dog musher *extraordinaire!* Hee Yawwww!

Day 50, November 3 (Low -10, High 10, cloudy)

It's nice to be back "home." The river is really overflowing. The channels that have been frozen for weeks are now covered with a blue slush moving slowly downstream. If this keeps up the whole riverbed, which is anywhere from a quarter- to a half-mile wide including the various channels and river bars, will be a flat expanse of ice.

I have embarked on a project to bring more light to the cabin. (Actually, it would be more accurate to say that I am using and re-using all the light that is available.) Cluttered with a combination of Reynolds Wrap, pieces of shiny tin, silver stovepipe, and a weird assortment of lamps, lanterns and candles, the place is beginning to look like the midway of an old carnival. I'm determined to fight the absence of sunlight, which is now down to about six hours on, eighteen hours off.

I may have written this elsewhere in this journal but it bears repeating: The single most important impact on me during my first winter in Alaska, in the sub-Arctic, not the Arctic, which is more intense, was not the cold, but the absence of daylight. You can prepare your body for the cold with proper clothing, but it's hard to get your psyche to anticipate the effect of all that darkness.

Day 51, November 4 (Low -5, High 10, cloudy)

I baked my second loaf of bannock (pan bread) today. The first was under Mike's supervision at his fish camp a couple of days ago. (Whole wheat flour, cooking oil, dry milk, water, and yeast — optional — for taste. Cook in a frying pan or skillet, one side with lid, other without. Not exactly baking, but it's quick and good.)

I took the last of the available wood from the "bear tree" today. From now on wood foraging will be downriver and cross-river.

There was a message for Mike and me this evening on a radio program called "Trapline Chatter." It was from a couple we both know who work at Denali Park, but who are this year for the first time in memory spending the winter in the Lower Forty-Eight. Normally at the end of the tourist season they load their gear and dogs into a plane and fly off into the Arctic for the winter, to a place in fact not too far from here.

"Trapline Chatter" may require a brief explanation: There are a number of radio stations in Alaska that have similar programs, but Trapline is probably the best known simply because it emanates from one of the most powerful radio stations in Alaska and reaches most of the northern half of the state. The station is KJNP (King Jesus North Pole, a religion-sponsored station, naturally, and the reason the FCC has seen fit to give it such a loud voice, wattage wise. It is located in the little town of North Pole, not far from Fairbanks.) and the program is simply one of messages. All kinds of messages. An electronic bulletin board of the North. Listening to "Trapline Chatter" every evening from the snugness of my warm cabin, I learn that a certain Arctic river is overflowing and temporarily dangerous to travel on; which passes are impassable; where a food cache is waiting to be picked up; whose baby has been born, and who has died; what family at Anaktuvuk Pass hopes to spend Thanksgiving with an even more isolated family somewhere in the Brooks Range. There is of course drivel aplenty, but Arctic flavor even in that.

Day 52, November 5 (Low -10, High 5, clear)
   This was one of those times that make the cloudy Arctic days worth enduring. Crisp (very crisp), clear, and short (very short). On days like this the Arctic, strangely enough, reminds me of the desert, in spite of the snow and ice. Looking south I can see until the earth curves out of sight below the horizon. North, the near-frozen river hides its source in the folds of the Brooks Range.

Day 53, November 6 (Low -5, High 10, cloudy)
   Lots of overflow but the main channel is still open. Places to get water are getting farther away and more scarce.
   The trouble with being a long way from medical help is that you tend to "psych" yourself out with every little pain. Right now I've got a strange pain in my side: Pleurisy? Sprained muscle? Bruised rib? I dunno.

Day 54, November 7 (Low -5, High 20, cloudy)
   Tropical! I was out cutting wood today when it became apparent that I was getting uncomfortably warm, an unusual occurrence recently. A glance at the outdoor thermometer told me why. It was twenty above. If my record-keeping is accurate, the last time it was this warm was on October 16.
   In response to the balmy weather the river has put on a spectacular display of overflow. Out in front of my cabin the river now looks like a vast lake, more than a quarter-mile wide. Still left, bisecting this "lake," is one channel of open water constricted to only a few feet in width, a horizontal waterfall in both sight and sound.
   I fell from grace last night. Some time in the middle of the night I awoke to the sound of a B.F.C. doing the shrew dance on a piece of Reynolds Wrap I had left lying on the counter. His beat was so compulsive I began pounding it out with a spoon. Unfortunately in my enthusiasm I tapped the little bugger on the head, thus

inadvertently assisting the late-night terpsichorean on his journey into the void.

Day 55, November 8 (Low 5, High 33, windy)

The temperature hovered somewhere between thirty-two and
thirty-three today, making this two-day hot spell the warmest
since October 11. It is positively stuffy around here. I'm rapidly
learning that once acclimated to subzero temps, anything above
that becomes uncomfortable in more ways than one: The snow
gets rather mungy; the eves begin dripping meltwater; the trees
become bare; the river overflows and becomes temporarily
impassable; and the world around me seems to lose its precise,
clean crispness.

The mysterious malady I am entertaining is still a mystery. I
have ruled out any rib damage because, in spite of much poking
and probing, I can't elicit any pain tactually. There is also no
outward sign of bruising. But there is considerable pain when I
cough, when I try to pick something up with my right hand, and
when I chop or saw wood. The pain seems to be centered around
the right lung, sometimes in front, sometimes in back, and usually
high. Which would seem to lean in the direction of pleurisy.
Unfortunately, *The Complete Medical Guide*, a large volume for
which I joined The Book of the Month Club this past summer, and
hauled up here in lieu of five pounds of coffee, raisins, chocolates,
or some *useful* food, is somewhat less than complete. The entire
entry on the subject of pleurisy states: "Pleurisy is an inflamma-
tion of the Pleura. Its main symptom is pain when you take a deep
breath." Some help!

Day 56, November 9 (Low 5, High 20, sunny)

The humidity must have gone up along with the temperature
because even though it's thirty to forty degrees warmer, it still
feels about as cold as when it was twenty below.

The villagers of Kobuk, an Eskimo village on the Kobuk River
in this part of Alaska, are very democratic. They set some kind of
record in a special run-off election yesterday when twenty-five of
twenty-six registered voters voted. Shishmaref, another Inupiat-
speaking village located on the Seward Peninsula southwest of
here, displayed some flexibility by voting to make booze illegal

there. In the space of less than a year, the village has voted booze out, in, and back out again!

Day 57, November 10 (Low 5, High 20, clear)
There is a certain amount of intellectual and physical lassitude around here today. I'm going to have to force myself into some venture or sink into a mire of ennui. A blizzard would be a little diversion.

Day 58, November 11 (Low 5, High 15, cloudy)
Mike is back. He says he will be around until the first week in December, when he will go to the village for commercial dog food to augment the poor fish catch. I will try to write a few letters to go out with him. He is going to spend several weeks in Fairbanks around the Christmas holidays, and I have agreed to sit his dogs if needed. Actually he would prefer to leave them with somebody in the village so when he returns he won't be dependent upon the vagaries of flight to get back here.

I have already mentioned "Trapline Chatter," the radio message program on KJNP, North Pole. KOTZ at Kotzebue has a similar program. There is a difference in content, however, and the difference has just come to me. KOTZ's messages are mostly from and to Natives. KJNP's missives, on the other hand, are mostly to and from non-Natives. This disparity is not necessarily geographical. People like Doug, Christy, Mike (and now me), although closer to Kotzebue, listen to KJNP.

Day 59, November 12 (Low 5, High 15, cloudy)
Don Schmuckel showed up today. His arrival has been rumored for some weeks now. He'll be staying in a cabin upriver, but expects to go Outside for a couple of months around Christmas. He's a former junior high teacher from Michigan who, like most of us, is in Alaska looking for something. He spent much of last winter running a small general store in the village. Last summer he had a unique job with the National Park Service, unique for anywhere but Alaska, that is. Alaska has a whole raft of new National Parks, most of them roadless, without facilities, accessed only by boat, plane or foot. Don worked at Kobuk National Park, patroling and to some extent noting and identify-

ing what was in the park, because at that point the contents of the park were still somewhat of a mystery to its administrators.

Don had been waiting patiently for a charter flight to fly him and his supplies up here, but the availability of the plane and pilot, and good weather never seemed to coexist. Finally, he got tired of waiting and hired someone to bring him as far upriver as they could get with a snow machine towing a dogsled loaded with supplies.

They got as far as Mike's fish camp before overflow stopped the snow machine cold. For the past three days Don has been pulling and pushing the dogsled, sans dogs, upriver. Today he hiked up from Six-mile with nothing more than a rifle and a Thermos. Mike has offered to take his dogs down tomorrow and bring his supplies up. It was so crowded with three of us up here that I was overcome with my social obligations and ended up doing nothing else!

Day 60, November 13 (Low 5, High 20, cloudy)

I have been reflecting (you are not entitled to do that until after age fifty, and then only occasionally) on my conversation with Don yesterday. With so many altruistic people who come to Alaska, including me, Mike, Don, and most people I have met who live in the bush, the topic of conversation soon turns to Natives and Native culture. Don, based on his village store experience, said he had counted nine different kinds of government checks that Natives regularly cashed there. He was making the point that real subsistence living on the part of Natives is at least partially ephemeral. (The biggest-selling food item in his store was Banquet frozen fried chicken.) Most round-eyes up here, including Don, regret what has happened to Eskimo culture and would like to see it change back, as would many Eskimo elders, but that isn't very likely. Many urban Alaskans, on the other hand, talk about Natives the way native Americans were generally characterized a century ago in the Western U.S.

These transplanted Lower-Forty-Eighters (as aren't we all) are here for the buck. They venture into the bush once a year, if that often, to shoot at moose and tin cans, but then only behind the protection of tanklike vehicles and other all-terrain oddities. To them *all* Natives are drunks; they resent the unfair competition that Natives (and wolves) represent in the pursuit of their "sport," and their attitude toward their fellow man in this so-called enlightened age is only a step removed from "the only good Indian is a dead Indian."

There is a basic paradox, even with "bush" people. Most round-eyes in the bush want to live the way the Natives used to — with some very big exceptions, including access to the Outside for friends and relatives, medical aid *and* supplies. Most of them, like me, want to work relatively briefly for good money. Natives want what we have already had, and to some extent rejected. The paradox is very visible in local transportation in the villages. There is hardly a Native dog musher left in Alaska. (That's an overstatement, but not by much.) Natives want snow machines and ATV's. Round-eyes, living in the bush and in the villages, are more and more opting for dog teams. The Iditarod Race from Anchorage to Nome, "The Last Great Race," may have as many as fifty or sixty entrants, but less than a handful are Natives.

Day 61, November 14 (Low -5, High 10, clear)

Exquisite! "Delicately or poignantly beautiful" is one defini-tion of the word. And the word is a perfect description of today. Delicate, because each day now is all too short. (Because this is a north-south valley, sunrise is now about eleven-thirty forenoon and sunset at three in the afternoon, the sun never more than a few degrees above the southern horizon.) Poignant, because the beauty is literally breathtaking. As I went to cut wood this morning, each birch tree was a small miracle. The white bark peeling away from the slender trunks was frozen sculpture; frost, collected on branches absent of leaves, melted into hundreds of glistening diamonds when struck by sunlight. On top of the frozen overflow, where I was walking, were crystals of frost formed in the shape of tiny feathers.

At the end of the day I went out over the ice to the last remain-ing open channel, less than a yard wide, to fetch water. The overflow was a blaze of yellow in the sunset. In the northern distance, peaks of the Brooks Range were bathed in alpenglow. Entranced, I set the water container down and did a slow pirouette. Finally, and reluctantly, I made to leave and found the water container frozen fast to the ice, a seemingly permanent part

of the landscape, which required a trip to the cabin for an ax.

Late in the evening a half-moon repeated, almost too perfectly for belief, the sun's earlier trajectory.

Day 62, November 15 (Low 0, High 10, clear)

Prowling around in the food cache, I discovered two full-sized caribou hides which prompted me to do some interior decorating. The bed is in one corner of the cabin, so I decided to "wallpaper" the two adjoining walls with the hides, which have very nice contrasting areas of brown and white. If it works, the bedroom should be attractive both visually and tactually.

The next project after the bedroom will be to cover a five-gallon kerosene can with some kind of material for a stool or ottoman.

Day 63, November 16 (Low -5, High 5, clear)

It has been close to a month and a half since we have had any appreciable snowfall. What fell before is still here but it is getting kind of grungy, especially around the cabin. We need another foot or two!

The caribou skins are up on the "bedroom" walls, and some of the ceiling too for good measure. That part of the cabin is now like a furry cocoon. Looks nice, and feels good too.

I have discovered where the B.F.C.s have been dining: in the soda cracker box! As long as the crackers last, they can have it with my blessings. I had not been able to imagine what the B.F.C.s were doing to make such a racket. Well, it appears that they get into this cracker box, which is sort of like an echo chamber because it is nearly empty, and then start nibbling at the cellophane-wrapped crackers. Translating what they must hear from inside, based upon what I hear outside, that cracker box must be their version of the Rolling Stones at Altamont.

Day 64, November 17 (Low -5, High 5, north wind)

I completed the transformation of a kerosene can into a stool and, worrying about hyperactivity, called it a day.

Day 65, November 18 (Low -5, High 5, cloudy)

Mike and I crossed over the river today looking for water and wood. It is an eerie feeling to walk over and look down at a stream beneath your feet that only a few days ago was noisy and bubbling —now silent and covered with several inches of ice through which you can see clearly the round-pebbled bottom.

We found open water directly across from my cabin, and spotted a number of standing dead spruce trees in the area. The temperature hovered around zero, but a north wind of twenty to thirty mph put the chill factor 'way below that. My nose turned white from frostbite, which caused me a little anxiety, even though at that stage the cure is quick and easy. Just take your glove off and cup your bare hand over the afflicted part for a few seconds, and the circulation will return. The trick is not to let it go on too long, in which case serious damage can be done. With more than one person, it is standard practice to check each other out visually every once in awhile, a kind of Arctic buddy system. When I'm by myself, I find myself going through all kinds of weird facial contortions to see whether any portion of my exposed face feels numb. It probably looks strange, but it works. The parka I'm wearing for really cold weather is made from goose down, extends down to my knees, and has a hood with a fur ruff. The ruff holds a pocket of air in front of the face, and except when there is a wind, like today, is usually sufficient protection. Like so many things here in the Arctic, frostbite is just one more thing you have to pay attention to *all* the time.

I'm cooking chili for the neighborhood tonight.

Day 66, November 19 (Low 0, High 15, cloudy)

Almost a month has passed since the grizzly incident. I have been carrying my rifle outside the cabin ever since. Today, after lugging the gun plus towing a wood-laden sled across a thousand or more yards of super-slick ice, I decided that caution could very well degrade into paranoia. From now on I'm going to leave the gun behind. The simple fact of carrying it tends to color the wilderness experience, so I'm going to quit doing it and think positive. Besides, according to bear theorists, all *Ursus arctos horribili* should now be in their dens.

Tonight I'm going to attempt to sew a round pillow cover for the kerosene-can footstool. I have been reading recently about subatomic particle theory as defined by Quantum Mechanics (from a great book entitled *The Dancing Wu Li Masters*). Subatomic particle theory seems downright simple when compared to the knowledge required in negotiating successfully the tucks and folds encountered in the topological art of round-pillow sewing.

Day 67, November 20 (Low 0, High 15, cloudy)

I got down to serious across-the-river woodcutting today. I found two large, dead spruce trees right next to each other. So close, in fact, that when I tried to drop the first, it hung up on the second, and I had subsequently to fell them both at the same time. I don't like to do that because it creates too many variables that can go wrong. Just cutting down dead trees is bad enough. In logging country they call dead trees "widow makers." Two of them together would more appropriately, it seems to me, be called "suicide."

On the way back to the cabin with the first sled-load, rejoicing at the successful felling of both trees, I broke through the ice which bridged a small inlet. Luckily the water was only thigh-deep, but the muddy bottom was like quicksand. Fortunately I was wearing waders, so I didn't have to race to the cabin with freezing feet. But I had broken through the only ice bridge crossing the inlet, so I had to carry each piece of wood through the gluelike mud and reload the sled on the other side.

Last night I awoke, looked out the window, and saw a marten looking right back at me. Later he tore some moss from between two of the wall logs, but finally gave up on that and left. I will have to disabuse him of any further moss predation. I'll need all the moss I have when it gets fifty below!

Day 68, November 21 (Low 5, High 25, snow)

Two or three inches of snow fell during the night. It's much easier, I discovered, to pull a loaded sled over bare ice than ice lightly covered with snow. No traction. The snow particles act like tiny ball bearings on the ice.

A couple of chickadees came by to watch me cut wood in the lightly falling snow. There are at least two other species of small birds that stay here over the winter: the red poll and the red-headed crossbill. About a month ago I saw a spruce grouse near the cabin. The ubiquitous ravens are around most of the time, if not seen, then heard. Plenty of gray jays, but I have yet to see the Alaska State bird, the ptarmigan. Today I spotted a bird that I have just now identified from my *Audubon Bird Guide*. It's called the dipper, and according to the guide it feeds in open streams. I spotted it near an open lead of water where I now go for my drinking water.

Day 69, November 22 (Low 15, High 30, snow)
Light snow fell most of the day. The phrase "most of the day" is no longer operative (as Nixon used to say), because it could now mean as little as two or three hours. With the low clouds today, it seemed as if it started getting dark at about the time it started getting light.

The other day I had a brilliant idea for a candle holder, part of my ongoing program entitled "let there be light." I cut the bottom out of a square five-gallon can, leaving about three inches of the side intact. The inside of the bottom and sides is a shiny silver color, good for light reflection. Then I nailed it to the wall in the configuration of a diamond. Using wax as solder, I fabricated a little tin platform on which to set the candle. Nice conceptual approach to problem-solving. But it didn't work. What I invented was not a candle holder, but a candle oven. With all that tin surface radiating heat back at the cabin, a six-hour candle becomes a puddle of wax in about ten minutes. Maybe I'll use my candle oven for baking very small cookies.

Day 70, November 23 (Low 10, High 25, snow)
Mike came by today to reaffirm that we're having Thanksgiving dinner at his place tomorrow. Sweet and sour caribou, I'm told. I'm baking blueberry pie for the occasion. It would be nice if it could be said that I had cleverly picked the berries this fall and preserved them in an ice pit 'til needed. But I didn't. I bought a can of pie filling last September.

About a half-foot of snow has fallen in the past few days. The carpet around the cabin is once again a pristine white.

Day 71, November 24 (Low 10, High 20, cloudy)
Thanksgiving Day
Author's note: My original and only entry under this date was

a rather curt "Thanks, but no thanks." In retrospect I believe this was meant to be an editorial commentary on the current phoniness of most national holidays, rather than a critique of Mike's cooking. The sweet and sour was excellent, as was Mike's home-baked rye bread, shared by Don, Mike and me. We made snow ice cream to go with the blueberry pie and, in general, just plain stuffed ourselves.

Day 72, November 25 (Low 5, High 10, north wind)
First day of Christmas shopping. I gotta get to a shopping mall right away!

Day 73, November 26 (Low 0, High 10, cloudy)
In the continuing battle to utilize whatever light is available, I instituted the white sheet maneuver. This was accomplished by taking an old sheet I found up in the food cache and stapling it to the ceiling, thus utilizing (but not gaining) an estimated ten foot-candles of illumination being sucked into the smoke-darkened ceiling.
I have not used the workshop except for storage, so today I belatedly decided to use it as a woodshed. Why this thought did not visit me earlier is somewhat of a mystery. I'm going to stack it full of split wood ready to go into the stove. I put about a quarter cord in today.
We're down to less than five hours of "workable" daylight.

Day 74, November 27 (Low 10, High 20, snow)
We have added eight to ten inches of snow in the last two or three days. The old snow is compact now, so the total is still only about a foot deep. I have to continually re-remind myself not to knock the snow off my boots by kicking trees, because the spruces are loaded with snow and it takes only a slight jar to trigger the dumping mechanism. In fact, you can watch the arboreal progress of a red squirrel without even seeing the creature simply by following the succession of snowfalls from tree after tree.
I went for a long walk on the river tonight after dark. Snowing, quiet, eerie. I should have done that on Halloween.
If the wind doesn't blow all the snow off the ice, wood-gathering (or rather, sled-hauling) is going to be difficult.

Day 75, November 28 (Low 15, High 30, snow)

Busy Day! I was out splitting wood around noon when the report of a rifle shot from the direction of Mike's cabin began ricocheting back and forth between the mountains. It seemed as if it took five minutes for the echoes to stop. Ahah, I thought, either Mike has got some "meat" or he has finally decided to shoot Mowgli, the young sled dog who refuses to pull. After checking the river for anything that might have run out of the trees, I went back to cutting wood. A second shot, with hardly an echo, convinced me that Mike had just performed a *coup de grace* on something bigger than a dog. Sure enough, Mike showed up a few minutes later and asked me to help him butcher a moose. He had been on his way to my place for a cup of hot chocolate when he came onto fresh sign. He dropped the moose, a cow, about midway between his cabin and mine. We had to snowshoe into where the moose was lying, looking a little like a collapsed barn. I see them every day at Denali in the summer, but until you touch one, even a dead one, you can't possibly judge their size. This one must have weighed twelve hundred or thirteen hundred pounds, and would dress out at seven hundred or eight hundred pounds, which pretty much takes care of the winter meat supply. We skinned it, gutted it, quartered it, and hauled it to Mike's with the dogs. It took two sled-loads to get it there. The whole operation took about five hours, and it was quite dark when we finished. We were both covered with blood and gore, especially Mike, who had practically crawled inside the stomach cavity to get the intestines out. The moose was very fat, so the dogs will be happy for awhile.

I had planned on making a water run sometime today, but will melt snow instead.

Day 76, November 29 (Low 15, High 32, clearing)

As I write this at about eight in the evening, the temperature has dropped and the snow feels its normal crispness underfoot. Earlier today it was mushy, an unusual texture for Arctic winter snow. The sun appeared briefly in midday and set the mountains aglow with a glorious pink light. It was almost a combination sunrise/sunset, which we will see in about a week if the weather is clear. Around December 7 the sun will go down for the last time this year and not reappear until about mid-January.

Mike came over again today and saw three caribou drifting through the spruce trees. After yesterday he is apparently feeling a surfeit of meat, because he did not go back and get his gun. Animal traffic, ruminant variety, is on the upswing.

Day 77, November 30 (Low 15, High 25, clear)
Apparently we are to be treated with a series of spectacular "sun shows" before it exits the Arctic scene. Today the sunset went on for about two hours. I had to stop chopping wood every fifteen minutes to watch it.

Still trying to differentiate between a real wilderness experience and what the vast majority settle for, I have decided that true pleasurable experiences might be one measurement. Here, whatever pleases you connects with some personal, inner motivation; a sunset, a found spruce tree, an animal sighting. What most "normal" people see as pleasurable is what they are told is pleasurable; a diamond ring, a second car, designer jeans, a new hairdo.

On the way to cut wood I saw a small martenlike animal crossing the wide part of the snow-covered river. Whatever the animal was, you could tell it felt exposed and didn't waste any time getting off the open area and into the trees.

December

Day 78, December 1 (Low 5, High 20, clear)
Sunrise, woodcutting, sunset.

Day 79, December 2 (Low 5, High 20, cloudy)
I had to wake up early this morning to get a couple of letters to Mike before he left for the village. I resuscitated an old wind-up alarm clock to wake up by. As a consequence I spent the night dreaming terrible dreams of flashbacks to previous occupations where alarm clocks were needed. Tough.

Day 80, December 3 (Low 5, High 15, cloudy)
A Native lady drowned in the Kuskokwim River yesterday when her three-wheeler (an all-terrain vehicle that looks like a fat, motorized tricycle) went through the ice during a warm spell. The non-Native announcer at the Dillingham radio station, from whence I received this sad information, ended his report by warning his listeners (a large percentage of whom are Natives) to beware of the dangerous ice conditions.

This was a warning I feel would have been superfluous a decade or so ago. For the last ten thousand years or so, Native Alaskans have known the dangers of rivers during warm-ups in winter. The fairly recent advent of three-wheelers and other ATV's seems to have caused a short circuit in genetic message transmission.

Day 81, December 4 (Low 5, High 20, light snow)
Today was a day of re-trenching. I hardly left the cabin. I caught up on laundry and sewing and rearranged the radio antenna. I can

now get about three additional stations. "About" because reception is always problematical.

Day 82, December 5 (Low 10, High 25, cloudy)
Some geographical contrast on a day when Arctic ennui seems to be creeping up on the cabin. South of the sub-Arctic one can afford to put off today's wood-gathering and water-collecting for some indefinite time in the future. Here, it's get wood or freeze, get water or die!

Day 83, December 6 (Low 10, High 25, cloudy)
Today was supposed to be the last day of potential direct sunlight this year, but we will never know because it was too cloudy. A famous quotation warns, "Do not go gentle into that good night." The author, Dylan Thomas, was speaking of death. I don't have the same concern for the long night I am facing, because I know there is sunlight at the end of the time tunnel, but not, alas, for more than a month. When the sun comes back up it will be the other side of winter solstice, each day will be getting longer, and we'll be on that long downhill slide into Arctic spring!

Day 84, December 7 (Low 5, High 10, clear but no sun!)
Some of the messages of KJNP's "Trapline Chatter" (and other stations such as those in Point Barrow, Kotzebue, Nome, etcetera) are worthy, it seems to me, of preservation. For example, here's one that has been running the last two nights, as near verbatim as I can recall it: "Going out to Dolores Nukpuk at Arctic Village from the North Star Borough Land Office: 'We are in receipt of an overdue property tax notice in your name. If we do not receive payment in the amount of two hundred and forty dollars and eight cents by January 1, said property will be subject to auction in lieu of back taxes. Have a very, very merry Christmas.' "
If I am permitted to editorialize here, I would have to say the second "very" borders on extreme cruelty, a linguistic twisting of the knife blade, as it were.
There is a lady from the Pacific Northwest who "writes" to her daughter and son-in-law in the bush via KJNP nearly every day. If her recitals are anywhere near true (I have slowly come to the opinion that she is certifiably crazy) she leads the most incredibly

negative life possible. Something *bad* is always happening to her, from an overflowing bathtub to an evicting landlord, from a seized rental truck — loaded, of course, with all her earthly goods — and a "ransom" set at five thousand dollars, to a whole series of conflicts with government agencies who are trying to help her. Her latest: She now has three jobs, but not enough income. "Love, Mother."

Day 85, December 8 (Low -5, High 2, clear)

Now hear this! The superintendent of the Anchorage Municipal Jail was arrested yesterday for shoplifting.

Today was the first clear day (absolutely clear) since the sun went down more or less permanently. To the south there were seven thousand shades of pink, and everywhere the mountains were draped in alpenglow.

Day 86, December 9 (Low -10, High -5, clear)

The shallow, horizontal light from a sun that "isn't" makes for some strange visual effects. The trails that I and others, including animals, have made since the last snow stand out in silhouette on the flat, frozen river like the mysterious (Aztec?) markings in South America that can be seen only from aircraft.

This afternoon I spotted Don hiking along the river from his cabin. As with a mirage on a desert, it was almost impossible to tell whether he was coming toward me or going away. I watched for about five minutes until I was sure, then went in and put the kettle on for coffee.

Day 87, December 10 (Low -15, High -10, clear)

More than thirty percent (33-1/3 to be exact) of the upper river population will leave the area tomorrow. Don is going Outside for Christmas and does not plan to return, he says, until February at the earliest. Mike is going out later for Christmas in Fairbanks, but will not be gone so long. On the sly, I had Don carry a letter for me to KJNP. Mike is always complaining that he never gets any messages on "Trapline Chatter." So, this Christmas when he is in Fairbanks, he will get a message from here, a switch he should appreciate.

The weather continues very cold and very clear. And very, very beautiful. It is so cold and quiet, I sometimes feel I'm seeing things, not like a motion picture, but as a series of still freeze-frames. Click, click, click.

At fifteen below today I decided not to go on a wood expedition. The workshop-cum-woodshed is about full, so from now on, unless the mood strikes me otherwise, when the temperatures are very low I'm going to say the hell with wood-gathering. As noted earlier, you can safely do that only when your wood supply on hand is fat city.

Day 88, December 11 (Low -15, High -10, clear)

I have been trying for more than a dozen years to kick the Protestant work ethic, but so far have not succeeded. Sometimes I think I have finally done it, only to have a major relapse. This is the second day in a row I have *not* ventured out to get wood. The "woodshed" is full, the temperature is fifteen below, I *don't* need any wood, and I still feel tremors of guilt for my inactivity. If I could transfer this feeling (or sublimate it) to my typewriter, I would be pleased. But no, so tomorrow is to be a wood and water day.

Day 89, December 12 (Low -20, High -10, clear)

Guilt and morbidity over the work ethic are no longer viable. Mike came by last night and asked whether I would like to assist in a logging expedition. Anything for a change. So today we felled, bucked, limbed and peeled a number of straight spruce trees, the logs to become the south wall of Mike's new workshop. Tomorrow or the next day we'll haul them in with the dogs.

Speaking of the latter, Mike spotted some dog feces with worms last night, which necessitated that this morning he begin sticking pills the size of walnuts down dog throats. One pill per ten pounds of body weight, which translates into a minimum of four pills per dog. Puss, who weighs at least sixty pounds, must have figured the mathematics in advance, because he resolutely refused to open his mouth and Mike had to resort to a stick as a pry-bar for each of the six pills.

Day 90, December 13 (Low -20, High -10, clear)

I'm becoming an accomplished "drawknifeman." Hardly a log

cabin would have been built in Alaska (or anywhere else, for that matter) without the drawknife. It's a very simple tool; a blade on each end of which are gripping handles, the whole tool more or less the shape of a right-angled U. It can be used to sculpt a whole variety of items made from wood, including canoe paddles, all sorts of handles from hammers to hoes, and even kitchen stirring spoons. But I'm using it for something much more mundane; scraping the bark from spruce logs for Mike's workshop. It's nice to be doing something purposeful, I guess, but on the other hand, that sounds suspiciously like a statement a prot-work-eth would make.

I think working at ten or fifteen below takes more acclimation than I have attained so far. It doesn't seem to affect Mike, but after a few hours of not-very-hard work, I am exhausted.

Mike has embarked on a program of capturing and killing B.F.C.s with mouse traps baited with almonds. How *gauche*.

Day 91, December 14 (Low -15, High -10, clear)
Peach! For almost a week I have been trying to find the proper word to describe the predominant color that appears in the south in place of the missing sun. Peach!

I brought the bearskin down from the food cache, where it has sat in a frozen, untidy bundle for the last two months. The head is still attached. I was planning to begin the tanning process by scraping and cutting off the pieces of meat and fat left on by my initial, rather frantic and unskilled skinning effort. But after about an hour of thawing I could see that the cabin was going to become a very gory and smelly mess before I could unfold the pelt and remove the head. So, I put it out in the woodshed where it immediately refroze, and where it will stay while I re-think the problem.

This incident was just another reminder to me of how incredibly clean and sanitary everything is up here as long as it stays frozen.

Most people would note this day as the eleventh day from Christmas. Not me. Because I pay attention, and am aware of such things (and occasionally listen to the Point Barrow radio station), I mark this day as the birthday of one Fanny Mae Bodfish of Barrow, Alaska. Long life, Fanny Mae!

©Dassow87

Day 92, December 15 (Low -20, High -10, clear)

Six days from winter solstice, ten days from Christmas, sixteen days from New Year's Eve, twenty-two days from sunshine!

From *The Keeners Manual:*

Minutes trudge
Hours run,
Years fly,
Decades stun,
Spring seduces,
Summer thrills,
Autumn sates,
Winter kills.

Day 93, December 16 (Low -15, High -10, cloudy)

Mike is heading out tomorrow for Christmas and New Year. In honor of his temporary Arctic exit I have baked a peach/strawberry Christmas pie. This may be both the first and last production of its kind. Mike will be replaced, as it were, by John Cooper, who has a cabin upriver, and who came by last night to drop off a package of Christmas candy mailed by my mother. The candy alone will make this rather bizarre Christmas seem like a real one. But reality stops there. Like the Chinese concept of Ying and Yang, love and hate, life and death, reality, it appears, must be balanced with unreality. Along with the candy came a note saying that Cathy, my daughter-in-law, is expecting in April, which means I shall emerge from the Arctic a grandfather, something I have never been before. I think I shall have to think about that.

Day 94, December 17 (Low 5, High 15, snow)

About six inches of fresh snow fell last night along with the advent of warmer weather. I put snowshoes on and broke the trail to Mike's (to borrow his *real* broom while he is gone). I also broke the trail across the river to the water and wood sources. Lots of fresh snowshoe hare tracks but no sign of the camouflaged creature that makes them. Plenty of marten tracks also.

Day 95, December 18 (Low 0, High 10, cloudy)

It's ten in the evening and I just returned from a full-moon hike on the river. A very nice substitute for the absent sun. The river was covered with a million glistening diamonds and the mountains were ethereal beyond belief! It was so exciting that I came back to the cabin, put a devils food cake into the "oven" and put a can of snow on the storm porch for snow ice cream when the cake would be ready. Postscript: chocolate cake, chocolate ice cream, and hot chocolate are rightfully redundant!

Bulletin: According to the late news, the ugliest hotel in the world has just burned down. (The news is via the radio; the architectural appellation is my own.) The hotel in question is/was the Jack Tar on Van Ness Avenue in San Francisco. In an apparent effort to disguise its ugliness the hotel name was changed from Jack Tar to Cathedral Hill Hotel in recent years, but that didn't work, so a quick conflagration may have been the most logical next step.

Day 96, December 19 (Low 0, High 30, clear, then cloudy)

Weird day. All day it had been cold, as it has been for weeks, it seems. Then about nine or ten this evening the temperature shot up to barely below freezing. The cause was a warm wind coming up from the south. I had hiked upriver in the moonlight, and when I returned the wind had nearly obscured my rather deep snowshoe tracks.

Day 97, December 20 (Low 10, High 20, clear)

Things are getting positively metaphysical around here. Today, around 2:30 p.m., the southern sky was doing a brilliant sunset, without benefit of the actual sun, of course, while the northern sky was framing a huge moon resting on the Brooks Range, so we had a simultaneous moon/sunset 180 degrees apart. The moon was as bright as the sun on a hazy day.

Addendum — A lesson in celestial mechanics: The moon was *not* setting when I saw it today at 2:30. It is now 9:00 p.m. and the moon has just risen in the East! Ergo: Either there are two moons, (an unlikely supposition, since surely the astronauts would have mentioned it in passing) or the moon does not "set" this time of year, but does what the sun does in summer in these latitudes. To wit, the moon rises behind the eastern mountains, arcs across the sky, and drops down behind the western mountains. Then it sneaks back to the east, low on the northern horizon, but not below it. I saw it this afternoon through a low gap in the mountains. All of this, I suspect, would have been perfectly obvious if I were out on the tundra of the North Slope, rather than enclosed in the grasp of the Brooks Range.

Day 98, December 21 (Low 5, High 15, clear)
   *This is it! WINTER SOLSTICE. Shortest day of the year! Exclaim! A time of great rejoicing for me, because from now on each day will have a little more daylight. In spite of the very cold temperatures to come, we are now on the long, glorious, downhill ride into Spring.
   Having now figured out the movement of the moon up here, I awaited patiently for it to appear through the gap of the Brooks Range as it did so spectacularly yesterday. It didn't.
   *(No, it isn't! According to the radio, winter solstice is not today, but tomorrow, the twenty-second. Well, what the hell. I'll have two consecutive days of rejoicing. You can't really over-rejoice, I always say.)

Day 99, December 22 (Low 10, High 20, partly clear)
   There is really no adequate way to describe the light up here recently. Imagine all the pastels you have ever seen and then add a few more. Probably the best description I have heard, although somewhat obtuse — and from more than one source, I might add — is when asked about the absence of the sun, the queried will reply, "Don't worry about it. The light that time of year is so fantastic you won't even miss the sun." True.
   Today was predominantly pink.
   My normally incredibly accurate tree-felling technique failed me today, due, no doubt, to an errant gust of wind rather than any failing on my part. In any case, the dead tree I was felling fell on a live tree and massacred the latter. When I looked at the corpse I realized that the very top — about three feet — was intended by the Tree Gods to be a yuletide decoration. I brought it home, put it in a sand-filled Crisco can (the sand being part of my standby stove repair kit), and it now sits *au naturel* next to my bed. Noel.

Day 100, December 23 (Low 10, High 15, clear)
   The light show continues in undiminished beauty. I look

forward every morning to what the day's display will be.

The BFCs are becoming arrogant again. Now that I have Mike's *real* broom I'm exploring dusky corners heretofore ignored, and there is BFC detritus everywhere. They are apparently in a nest-building furor. Because of the eminent arrival of the holiday season I have declared a temporary state of amnesty, but come next year, watch out!

I have read in some obscure publication fairly recently that there exists a species of BFC known as "the singing vole." If one of those dudes should appear in the next few days humming a bar or two of "White Christmas," I might consider an extension of the current peace accord.

Day 101, December 24 (Low 20, High 25, light snow)

John Cooper, who lives upriver a few miles, has decided, after all, not to go out for Christmas. He plans to race his dogs in the thousand-mile Anchorage-to-Nome Iditarod sled dog race in March and does not want to lose training time. His dogs are out of shape, and some of them have not yet recovered from the trip upriver a couple of weeks ago when they encountered icy conditions on the river that cut many of their feet. So, I shall not be sole King-of-the-River over the holidays, but since John has lived here for more than a decade, I'll be happy to share honors with him. I'm going to hike to his place this afternoon and will probably stay the night. I'll take blueberry pie filling and bake a pie up there as my contribution to Christmas dinner.

Day 102, December 25 (Low 10, High 30, cloudy)

Merry Christmas. Dinner at John's was moose steak, smashed potatoes and blueberry pie. John has a six-volt battery which is sufficient to run a tape deck for most of the winter, so we spent the day in a rather laid-back manner, listening to music, reading (me, a history of the Iditarod) and pigging out on food. We even had a tree, but never got around to decorating it.

Day 103, December 26 (Low -12, High -5, clear)

I stayed two nights at John's. Very pleasant. But today, on my return, my cabin was *very* cold. Two days without fire and the cold permeates everything. It took quite a few hours to re-warm it.

Which leads me into a brief discussion of a phenomenon which, for want of a better word, I shall call "log cabin glow." When you have had a fire going in a log cabin for awhile you can almost see the heat radiating back, or out of, the logs. A little molecular agitation, as it were. Now, if you talk to people who are knowledgeable about such things as insulation, and who speak in terms of R-factors and other engineering-type language, they will tell you, and correctly, I assume, that the log cabin is the worst-insulated structure in the history of the known world, or thereabouts. I can't argue that. But, I will say this: You can spend the rest of your life searching all the wood-frame, stone, brick, and/or whatever building materials you care to choose, and you will search in vain for a structure that has "log cabin glow."

Day 104, December 27 (Low -12, High -5, clear)
Direct sunlight bathed the very tops of the Brooks Range at midday, a promise of the sun's eventual return to those of us waiting patiently here in the Arctic.

Day 105, December 28 (Low -10, High -8, clear)
John is running out of dog food and is going in to the village to resupply tomorrow. He expects to be gone for less than a week. I will have the river to myself for a few days, after all. Well, almost. I have agreed to sit seven puppies, the mother of three of them, as they are still nursing, and two other injured adults. Today I built a shelter out of spruce limbs and snow for the puppies, even though John insisted that they can fend for themselves in thirty- and forty-below weather.

Lately I have been making meals out of brown rice and lentils, a combination which I think may prove addictive. It sure is filling, anyway. I don't seem to have either gained or lost weight even though I have been consuming vast amounts of sweets in cookies, cakes, pies, trail food, and most recently "mom's old-fashioned Christmas candy."

I read somewhere recently that the U.S. diet industry is collecting twenty billions of dollars annually from fattys who want to be skinnys. What a waste! All you have to do is round up a bunch of fattys, ship 'em up north, let them eat all they want for a couple of months, then ship them back south skinny as rails! No pain, no strain.

Day 106, December 29 (Low -5, High 0, clear, then snow)
Oh dear, oh dear, what can the matter be?
In one word: Responsibility!
I am now (and for the next few days) an incipient dog musher. My team consists of three adults: Dixie, Ace, and Buster, the latter two, injured, the former suffering from maternity; and seven no-name puppies, three of whom belong to Dixie and are still nursing.
Heavy duty! Food, medicine and worry. Not like the old days when the only adrenalin rush was a BFC scare.
John should be back in a week. In the meantime, it's just me, the river, and dogs, dogs, dogs.

Day 107, December 30 (Low 0, High 5, windy)
Based on a brief exploration around the cabin this morning, I believe I have discovered a flaw in the well-known basic law of physics called the conservation of energy (or maybe it's Isaac Newton's Law that for every action there is an equal and opposite reaction). Well, in any case, there appears to be much more coming out the rear of these dogs than I'm putting in the front! By the time I had shoveled and made one trip for water, daylight had come and gone.

Day 108, December 31 (Low -20, High -15, cloudy)
Happy New Year Dixie! Happy New Year Ace! Happy New Year Buster! Seven Happy New Years no-names! And uncountable Happy New Years to the BFCs of the world!

January

Day 109, January 1 (Low -20, High -15, north wind)

There was a cold wind blowing downriver all day. I went across the river to get water — usage has gone up considerably with the advent of "canine city." The temperature was fifteen below, coupled with a wind velocity of twenty-five or thirty mph must have put the wind chill factor out of sight. The dogs don't care, but I do, so I stayed inside and read most of the day.

Day 110, January 2 (Low -15, High -10, north wind)

For three days now I've been butchering a front quarter of the moose Mike shot. The untoward length of time is due partly to the fact that even a partial front quarter of a moose is a whole lot of moose, and in part because I know nothing about butchering, so I just keep hacking away until I hit bone. Some pieces of meat come out looking like steaks, sort of, so that's the way I'm treating them. Some pieces come off the bone looking rather forlorn and chunky, and those will eventually become mooseburger after being run through Mike's meat grinder. I'm wrapping all the meat individually in wax paper and storing it temporarily in the storm porch, where it freezes. Later it will go in the food cache. Radio messages from Mike and Don. The former expected back on the fifth, the latter, in February.

Day 111, January 3 (Low -5, High 2, snow)

Snow and wind today, so I had to re-break the trail to water and wood, which had drifted over and disappeared. The "trail," under these conditions, is more like a narrow, buried plateau snaking across the river. Even though, by now, I have made this trip literally hundreds of times, it is difficult to remember exactly where the trail is because the landmarks seem to change constantly. As a result each trail-breaking expedition is a kinetic adventure. If you put your snowshoe-clad foot down and it sinks in soft snow, you are off the trail; if it feels firm, you are on it!

Day 112, January 4 (Low -20, High -15, cloudy)
After one hundred and eleven nights of sleeping between the same two (and only) sheet blankets, I threw caution to the winds and washed them this morning. I hope I haven't been too hasty.

If Mike's celestial prognostications—made last November—are reasonably accurate, and if the weather clears, we should see the sun once again in about three days.

It has been so overcast since Christmas that there really hasn't been a sense of gaining daylight. But, from December 22 on, we, theoretically at least, have gained a couple of minutes of daylight each day.

Day 113, January 5 (Low -25, High 5, south wind)
I spent the night at John's. He had just returned from the village. He brought Scott McManus with him. Scott is the son of John's best friend, who was a schoolteacher in Ambler and a dog musher, killed in a plane crash while returning from the "Kuskokwim 300" race earlier this year. In Alaska, almost everyone you meet seems to have lost a relative or friend in a plane accident. Scott, in his early twenties, is going to the University of Alaska in Fairbanks, where he is studying to be a teacher.

John is going back to the village in two days to get more dog food, and I will take custody of the pups again. No adults this time.

Day 114, January 6 (Low -30, High -30, clear)
The coldest day so far, but no wind so it's not very noticeably different from ten or fifteen below unless you take a deep breath. If you do, you are immediately assailed with an apparent contradiction, because your throat feels as if it were on fire.

There is just a sliver of moon down south where the sun should be.

Day 115, January 7 (Low -15, High 0, light snow)

The seven puppies have returned, the three smallest—about six weeks old — without their mother this time. I guess I'll be surrogate mama for them the next few days. These three are friendly, cuddly, and love to come into the nice, warm cabin. The remaining four are something else. They hang around for food, steal it from the small puppies if I'm not watching, will not come into the cabin, and definitely will not be petted, or even touched. They are basically wild. The reason for this semiferal behavior, according to John, is that they were born this last summer when John was working on the North Slope and his dogs were being cared for and fed by a paid sitter in the village. The sitter ignored the newborn pups. Again according to John, pups have to be handled and gentled when they are very small and as they are growing up, or they will be basically wild. If John doesn't spend a lot of time with them between now and when they become adults, they won't be much good as sled dogs. You might, for example, be able to take them from their chain in the yard and put them in harness, but if they ever got loose, it would be almost impossible to catch them to put them back with the team. In the Iditarod this could be disastrous, because you must account for all of your team. If the dog is injured it can be brought to the next check point in the sled, but a dog running loose would probably lead to disqualification. So, using the feeding time as a kind of bribe, I'm trying to make friends, but so far without much success.

Day 116, January 8 (Low 0, High 2, cloudy)

Running short of paper birch — my version of oak for long, hot burning — I ventured downriver breaking trail with my snowshoes and pulling my little "red sled." (Years ago this type of cheap-plastic sled used to be red, although for lo these many years now it has been produced in a bright orange color. But, following the inevitable law of linguistic inertia, it is still called "the little red sled." For those without dogs it is the quintessential freight transport device in the Arctic.)

Anyway, about a quarter-mile from the cabin I began to get that feeling that I wasn't alone. I wasn't. When I turned around, I discovered there were seven small dogs single-filing quietly along behind me. My snowshoes had gone into the snow so deeply that

the three smallest pups couldn't see over the top of the sides of the trail. I chased them all the way back to the cabin because I didn't want them to think they could explore that far on their own. If a wind came up on the river, which it frequently does, the little pups could be put in mortal danger.

Day 117, January 9 (Low 0, High 0, cloudy)
More trips to the paper birch farm. This time the pups waited until I was out of sight and then followed my trail down to where I was cutting wood. They stayed quietly out of sight, apparently watching me work. When I returned to the cabin they were all sleeping soundly in a rather large puppy-pile. I would not have known of their unauthorized excursion, had it not been for seven perfect sets of tracks going down and back!

Day 118, January 10 (Low -5, High 0, clear)
More woodcutting, but the big news today was the reappearance of the sun after an absence of more than a month. As I was returning from woodcutting, pulling the loaded sled, heading north toward the cabin, I suddenly became aware of something warm caressing the back of my head. I turned, and there it was, a huge ball of orange, a horizontal sunrise moving from left to right emerging from behind a hill. I stood there letting the sunlight bathe my face, and the feeling was indescribably delicious. God, how I missed those warm, lovely rays. As I watched, the sun slid sideways from behind a low mountain to the south, traveled horizontally for a few minutes, and vanished behind another mountain. Here on January 10, sunrise is at 2 p.m and sunset at 2:15 p.m.

Day 119, January 11 (Low 0, High 15, cloudy)
Coming back from a cross-river expedition to get spruce (I had taken the four older pups and incarcerated the three fatsos for their own safety) the older pups began looking downriver expectantly. Since John was due back about then, I assumed it was he, but it was almost a half-hour before he came into view. (The pups are a very good early-warning system.) Actually, it was both John and Mike with their dog teams. Mike had gone on a twelve-mile round-trip to exercise the dogs and by chance had met John coming home. At a distance, on the snow-covered river, the two

dog teams and sleds looked like two slow-moving, dark lines followed by the exclamation points of the drivers standing on the rear sled runners.

John brought mail and, as he described them, "gifts" from the puppies. They were a dozen eggs and a sack of potatoes! Fresh food! Wow! Also a curious collection of mail forwarded from Toledo: junk mail from the International Cheese Lovers Club — junk mail in the Arctic. Bah. Bank statements, from which I learned I had more money in the bank than I thought I did. (Way to go, computers! Keep up the good work!) And lastly, a curious and rather sad letter, unsigned but designated as coming from a member of one of my tours of last summer. "I've never done anything as 'gutsy' as this before." It included a poem entitled "For Jim: You appeal to me . . . /you knew it, didn't you?/ your eyes looking back at me/sensed the need in mine/as I knew you felt alone too./ Then I think . . . /I'm not young,/I'm not pretty./ The great givingness in my soul/would not compensate./ How sad our hearts/ can't warm each other,/ our bodies move closely/ into a satisfying blend./ Why must each be alone/ when we each need another?"

Literary considerations aside, I defy anyone evolutionarily this side of a mountain gorilla to spend four months in the Arctic, read a letter like that, and remain dry-eyed. But, to get back on an even keel, "gutsy" would have been to sign it.

Day 120, January 12 (Low 20, High 30, snow)

Almost a foot of snow has fallen since last night and it is still coming down. It is also very warm, which I don't like. Doors start sticking, roofs begin leaking, and frozen things become unfrozen and yukky when temperatures climb. I prefer zero for the ideal winter day in the Arctic, a statement which may indicate both physiological and psychological acclimatization accompanied with just a touch of boreal bravado.

The pups have returned home so it will be quiet around here for a pleasant change.

Day 121, January 13 (Low 5, High 10, clear)

There have been a lot of fabulous days up here so far, but today must just about be the tops. A foot of fresh snow, a clear sky, an hour or more of pure sunlight, and in midafternoon, just as the sun set, a three-quarter moon which rose over the mountains to the east. No wind. Beautiful.

Now that the pups are gone the presumably resident marten left his tracks around the outside of the cabin last night. And the BFCs, quiescent for a week or more, were on the prowl again.

Day 122, January 14 (Low -10, High 10, clear)

Another beautiful day except for low clouds to the south, which partially obscured the sun. I went up to check on Don's cabin and found that some animal had trashed it. Not too badly, but silverware, dishes and canned food were knocked all over the place. I cleaned it up, and doing a Sherlock Holmes, decided the culprit was probably a marten whose track I could see going under the cabin, but I didn't discover how it managed to get inside.

I was visited by a creature last night — maybe the same one — who scratched around the outside enough to wake me, but not to get me up. I reasoned that if I invested enough energy in rising, I would have to kill the animal to balance things out, so not feeling particularly murderous, I stayed in bed and hammered on the wall. Eventually it left, leaving me with some really strange dreams for the rest of the night.

Day 123, January 15 (Low 10, High 15, cloudy)

I began thawing out the bearskin and head (again) in prepara-tion for de-fleshing and scraping. I did a lousy job of skinning in October but I may be able to save most of it. I have laid a piece of plastic on the floor to collect most of the gunk as it thaws, which will probably take at least a day.

Day 124, January 16 (Low 10, High 15, cloudy)

I helped Mike log today, so the bearskin and head are (again) back in the workshop re-re-freezing.

Day 125, January 17 (Low 10, High 15, cloudy)

Well, now. I got up this morning and almost immediately bumped my head on the lowest overhead roof beam, losing uncountable millions of brain cells in the process, and then proceeded to daub myself liberally with charcoal as I built the fire. (Each morning before rising I give myself the same speech: "OK, big fella, today you are not going to bump your head and you are not going to get smeared with charcoal.") Then, I patched a hole in some waders on loan from Mike, and as I was hanging them up afterward they caught on a nail and tore a huge hole farther up the leg.

Then, I went out snowshoeing and, getting the toe of one snowshoe caught under the other, I fell in complete disarray on an absolutely flat stretch of snow-covered river. It's rough, this Arctic living.

I am, of course, writing this from the safety of my bed, supine and unmoving.

Day 126, January 18 (Low 10, High 15, north wind)
We seem to be in a stable weather pattern the last few days. It's good for building up the wood supply so I can't complain. The bearskin is (finally) de-fleshed and de-headed. (Why do they say be-headed?) Next is scraping.

Day 127, January 19 (Low 0, High 10, north wind)
It was very, very windy today. The north wind blew all day at a velocity of thirty or thirty-five mph with a clear sky. It seems to me it should be a lot colder than it is. Maybe the winds presage a storm.

In the course of my wood-gathering today, I ran across a spruce tree that split like cedar. Oh joy!

Day 128, January 20 (Low -30, High -10, clear)
Ahah! Presience strikes again! Yesterday's wind was indeed a forerunner of a cold front. Today the river looks like a frozen sand dune sculpted by the wind. The trail across the river, once an indentation of compacted snow, is now a narrow ridge with the loose snow on each side of it having been blown away.

Speaking of snow, in the Inupiat language of the Eskimos there are something like two dozen words to describe different kinds of snow. Among them: *igluksaq*, snow-house building snow; *pukak*, snow granulated like sugar; *masak*, soft, wet snow; *ganik*, falling snow; *aput*, snow lying on the ground; *piqtuq*, snow being blown through the air in a ground blizzard; *aqilluqqaq*, firm snow; *mauya* soft, deep snow. The last being so phonetically descriptive it takes the breath away.

Day 129, January 21 (Low -5, High 0, windy)
Just when you have it figured out, it changes. Two days ago a north wind blew a cold snap into the valley. Last night the temperature dropped to minus thirty and the way it was dropping I expected minus forty or fifty this morning. Instead, a north wind blew during the night, and brought, not cold, but warm air, and this morning the temperature was back to zero.

This evening as I dumped the dishwater, I looked up and saw a star moving across the sky from south to north. Well, obviously not a star, I thought, but a satellite, more than likely Russian in that orbit. Suddenly, as I watched, another satellite appeared moving west to east and seeming to pass behind the first one. Star Wars? Beats me.

Day 130, January 22 (Low 0, High 0, windy)
Last night, it being Super Bowl Eve, the disc jockey at KJNP (King Jesus North Pole) played a record entitled "Kick Me, Sweet Jesus, Through the Goal Posts of Life," a nice and funny gesture, I thought, until after listening to a brief post-play commentary, I realized the DJ was multi-serious.

A tremendous pink afterglow lit the southern sky this evening, just after the sun had sidled behind Promontory Point.

Day 131, January 23 (Low -30, High -25, clear)
I went logging with Mike today in twenty-five-below weather. We dropped one tree on another and the latter shattered like glass. I felt like shattering, myself.

The seven puppies are back for a few days while John is traveling.

I suppose I should confine my reporting on events to those that take place here in the Arctic. A most important, significant, and symbolic occurrence, however, occurred yesterday far from here, in Salt Lake City. (I know about this for the same reason I knew about Fanny Mae Bodfish's Point Barrow birthday reported earlier.) It seems that yesterday a sixteen-inch waterline blew in

Salt Lake City when all the toilets in town were flushed at the same time at the beginning of Super Bowl half-time. The near universal demand for water caused a vacuum in the sixteen-incher, which promptly imploded.

Day 132, January 24 (Low -30, High -20, cloudy)

I have been killing paper birches with such regularity lately that I've forgotten that I have, indeed, been committing sylvan mayhem. Today, the puppies went with me to cut birch. As the tree I was sawing began to topple and fall, the pups let out yelps as if I were sawing on *them*, and ran all the way back to the cabin. Appropriate canine commentary.

Day 133, January 25 (Low -35, High -30, hazy)

I had to get water today in spite of the cold, and then decided as long as I was out I might as well cut some wood too. In doing so I learned again that one must pay attention in extreme cold. At one point I was adjusting my wool cap when my ungloved hand brushed my earlobe and I realized there was no feeling in it. In fact, my right earlobe felt like a stiff piece of cardboard. I held my bare hand on it until it began to get feeling back (and my hand began losing it), then made sure everything was covered while I was working. When I returned and entered the cabin I had about a half-pound of ice and frost on my face. As you exhale, your breath freezes immediately on whatever it strikes, mustache, beard, coat collar and cap front. The great Alaska myth is that heavy beards are some kind of protection against the cold. *Au contraire:* they are ice-collectors.

My single — one and only — chair disintegrated today from age and mildew, so I will have to build a new one. I'm thinking of constructing a combination chair/swing, but at this point have nothing more specific in mind.

Frost-bite bulletin: My ear is tender but still attached.

Day 134, January 26 (Low -43, High -30, ice fog)

I have always wanted to author an axiom like Socrates, Aristotle, et al. Now I think I have one: "When you go out woodcutting at forty below accompanied by seven sled dog puppies, indulge in restraint, keep calm, stay cool, and maintain an even temper at all times; otherwise, some future sled dog team may be running with empty harnesses."

Day 135, January 27 (Low -48, High -40, ice fog)
For reasons that are still not clear to me, I proved to myself, if not to others since there were no others present, that it is possible to fall and buck a tree, haul it, saw and split it, and stack it neatly while the temperature hovers at forty-five below zero. Why anyone would want to engage in proving such a postulate is and undoubtedly will remain a complete mystery.

Day 136, January 28 (Low -50, High -38, sunny)
Gettin' cold!
For the first time since early November there was enough sunlight that I could see most of the interior of the cabin without poking around with a flashlight! I hadn't realized how cavelike this place had become during the absence of *el sol*. Today it shone through the "kitchen" window and there were nice, yellow shafts of light bouncing off the walls, floor and sheet-draped ceiling. There has been a basic lighting dichotomy here for the past couple of months. During the so-called daylight hours it has been too light for lights, but not light enough without them.
A particularly noisy BFC has shown up in recent nights. If he — (sorry ladies) — If he, she or it perseveres in this behavior there may come an end to the amnesty which is now running nearly a month beyond expectations.

Day 137, January 29 (Low -48, High -40, clear)
The compacted snow on the trail crossing the river is now like a piece of leather stretched tightly over a drumhead. At least, that is my approximate simile. When you walk on it, it vibrates and echoes; and when seven puppies run along the trail, it sounds a little like a tiny troop of tympani playing diminuendo for the Philadelphia Philharmonic.
This morning the puppies were looking and listening intently in the direction of downriver, and I assumed it was John returning. In fact, I went out to the viewpoint where I could see a sticklike figure apparently moving back and forth across the river about a mile or so away. There was a heavy mist lying close to the ice,

obscuring the dogs and sled. Or, so I thought. After waiting a half-hour for someone to show up and nobody did, I decided the sticklike figure was probably a stick. (Followup: It was a sticklike figure, only it was Mike, not John, and he was going downstream, not up, which of course is why he never arrived at my place. Is this getting metaphysical? Or, just cabin-crazy?)

Day 138, January 30 (Low -40, High -36, clear)

I can sense a basic frustration looming up *vis-a-vis* me and the weather. With increasing daylight and the beautiful, clear, cold weather, this land cries out to be explored. But for me, it is too damn cold to do this with any degree of comfort for more than an hour or so. I guess I'll have to be satisfied with taking it in small doses. Too much exposure and even aesthetics freeze at forty below.

Day 139, January 31 (Low -50, High -44, clear)

The coldest day yet, but not too cold to get a load of paper birch, with the help of the Arctic Gypo Logging Company composed of myself and seven young members of the canine persuasion.

A cup of water on the kitchen counter froze solid last night, but the bed was warm.

February

Day 140, February 1 (Low -52, High -50)

Today's temperature: here, fifty-two below zero; in Ketchikan, forty-four above zero. I make that to be a ninety-six degree differential within the state on the same day.

I did a frostbite check while getting wood today, being extra careful in these very cold temperatures. (The very tip of my nose had almost no feeling, but I *think* it has always been that way. After all, how often in non-Arctic circumstances does one bother to measure the tactualness of one's nose?)

Everything froze inside the cabin last night. Everything, that is, except me. The repaired stove works fine, but because of air leaks I cannot bank a fire. If I try, it will smolder along until the middle of the night, when it finally combusts and I awake in a puddle of sweat.

Day 141, February 2 (Low -53, High -38, clear)

John returned today and took the puppies, so it is quiet around here for a pleasant change. John's and Mike's dog teams met downriver about a mile south of the cabin. As they were coming together, from my vantage point it looked like two primordial streams of steam approaching each other. In this extreme cold each dog exhales a breath that freezes immediately, leaving a collective cloud of mist trailing in the team's wake.

On the way upriver John saw a moose break through the ice, flounder for a few seconds and drown. Just like that.

Day 142, February 3 (Low -48, High -30, clear)

This was not a day of intense activity. Perhaps Arctic ennui is setting in. I did invent a good title to describe "knee-jerk" responses of whatever persuasion: "Gullible's Travails."

Day 143, February 4 (Low -50, High -38, clear)
John came by this afternoon looking for two of my former proteges, two of the older pups. They apparently followed John while he was on a training run and then made a wrong turn and got lost. About five p.m. the two pups literally staggered into the wood yard, and without a word (or a bark) collapsed into the lean-to I had built for the pups back when this all started, a couple of months ago. It's not good, I'm told, to feed the dogs right after a run, so I have waited two hours. In the meantime they have not moved a muscle.

Day 144, February 5 (Low -50, High -25, cloudy)
We're havin' a heat wave, a tropical heat wave . . .
I had breakfast for dinner today, but I didn't have dinner for breakfast, thus creating a certain amount of asymmetry.
Based on a semi-exhaustive survey of the literary contents of four cabins here on the river, two of which have been unoccupied for several years but still have intact paperback libraries — the most popular author here above the Arctic Circle appears to be Hermann Hesse; most popular novel, *Magister Ludi* by Hesse. Russians are big: Tolstoy, Gogol, Solzhenitsyn. Most popular American author, Kurt Vonnegut.

Day 145, February 6 (Low -45, High -25, clear)
The seven pups are back (they are still no-names). One is very sick with an unknown illness. I also have two limping adults, Missy and Sarah, taken out of action to recuperate for the Iditarod. I am giving the sick pup 200cc's of lactated ringers injection, 50cc's at a time. This is the first time I have ever used a hypodermic needle. I'm keeping the puppy inside, which should make the peripatetic BFC of recent nights sit up and take notice when he makes his nocturnal rounds tonight!

Day 146, February 7 (Low -40, High -20, clear)
The sick puppy is well, or at least he is eating again, which I take as a sign of wellness.

I painted a forget-me-not (the Alaska state flower) on a heart-shaped rock (which for verisimilitude I painted red). It is a birthday gift for downriver Anna.

Day 147, February 8 (Low -40, High -15, clear)
A significant canine event took place here on the river today. In most primitive societies some sort of ritual takes place when one of its members is deemed to have reached, chronologically or physically, a plateau known as puberty, adulthood, or something similar. Feathers and fur, bones and branches, mud and makeup, any or all may be employed to mark this momentous rite of passage. The largest of the young puppies, known by me as the tank because of his size and shape, for the first time today eschewed the squat and lifted his hind leg to urinate. This seems to me to rank in momentousness with any human change in status, and just as deserving of being recorded for history, which, in fact, is what I have just done.

The following has practically nothing to do with anything, although I feel there is a thread here somewhere. Anyway, one of the most bizarre titles I have ever come across was that of a sociological dissertation entitled, "The Sociological Aspects of Death as a Non-scheduled Status Passage." Really!

Day 148, February 9 (Low -40, High -20, clear)
John's back. Dogs are gone. The weather maintains.
The American Zoological Society has a standing offer of $50,000 to anyone who can provide proof of the existence of a boa constrictor or anaconda thirty feet long or longer. People have claimed to have encountered specimens forty, fifty, even sixty feet long. So why hasn't the award been collected? For the same reason, I suspect, that no one has ever collected a similar award offered by a Canadian gentleman to anyone who can prove that a human being has been injured or attacked by a non-rabid wolf. Fact and fiction in the animal world are far, far apart, especially with regard to large predators. Roll over in your grave, Jack London!

Day 149, February 10 (Low -35, High -20, clear)
Mike has been seeing lots of caribou sign south of here. Maybe

they are beginning to move back into this area, but I think it is much too early for the main migration northward through the Brooks Range and onward to the Arctic Slope.

Day 150, February 11 (Low -40, High -20, clear)
Looking for fire-starter this morning, I came upon a copy of a magazine called *McCalls*. The contrast between my life here and the super-gross consumption represented in the page after page of advertising is grotesque. It gave me the distinct feeling that I have, indeed, drifted into the backwater eddy of another world, psychologically and perhaps permanently.

Day 151, February 12 (Low -40, High -15, clear)
Sensory deprivation — temporary, of course — should be a mandatory experience. The silence here is so pervasive that the simple cry of a chickadee can be the signal for a joyful and profound celebration.

The sun is now arcing across the southern sky rather than sliding across the horizon as it was only a week or two ago.

Day 152, February 13 (Low -40, High -20, clear)
Don finally showed up, having left bits and pieces of gear scattered between here and the village. He left the village three days ago by snowmobile, but its owner refused to go farther than Doug and Christy's when he encountered overflow. Don's main supplies are stranded there. He pushed a small sled with about two hundred pounds of supplies a few more miles, but had to leave it, too. He staggered in here with only his backpack and snowshoes. Now he has to figure out how, short of a half-dozen trips on foot, he will get his gear up here. Maybe John can help him when he gets back.

Day 153, February 14 (Low -39, High -15, cloudy)
Three red crossbills perched for a minute or two on my ex-Christmas tree, which I had stuck in the snow at the end of the holiday season. The little tree had a good crop of cones, but the crossbills sampled a few and rejected the rest. Maybe they were too dry. All of a sudden there seems to be a lot more bird activity, although no new species have appeared.

Day 154, February 15 (Low -25, High -10, light snow)

I took Don over to see where I have been getting my water since the hole he had chopped and was using before Christmas is now frozen solid. Don, who is heavier than I, broke through some ice which I had just walked over. He got his feet only a little wet, but enough that he had to cold-foot it for home, on the double, as it were.

Day 155, February 16 (Low -50, High -22, clear)

Full moon last night. It was as bright as daylight at midnight. Today, at noon, the temperature was only twenty-five below, but in the afternoon it plummeted.

About four in the afternoon I fell through the ice just as Don did yesterday, only worse. Luckily I was closer to the cabin. By the time I reached it I was solid ice from the waist down. Had I been only a few miles from the cabin it would have been a life-threatening situation, and probably mortal without a blazing fire within minutes. But I made it to the cabin so fast I wasn't even chilled.

Day 156, February 17 (Low -48, High -35, clear)

I now have eight puppies for the next month and a half, while John prepares for and runs the Iditarod. As usual, John left late, after dark. He seems always to have last-minute things to do and almost never gets out of here in daylight. This time he returned within the hour. He had run into overflow in the dark, and he and his equipment got rather wet. He headed for home to dry out and will try again tomorrow, this time on the back trail, off the river.

Day 157, February 18 (Low -40, High -30, cloudy)

John left a six-volt battery to power my radio while he is gone. I hooked it up today but the radio will play only when I have the polarity reversed! That is, the negative lead on the positive terminal, and the positive lead on the negative terminal. Everything I know about electronics, which is close to zero, says this is nutty. Now, tonight, I can get only shortwave, not regular AM which I've been getting all winter. I dunno. I broke through the ice again, too!

Day 158, February 19 (Low -43, High -40, cloudy)

I broke through the ice *again*. I may very well be establishing a record for consecutive, involuntary Arctic immersions. The problem is that even though the weather has remained very, very cold, the ice near my water supply, over which I must cross, seems to be getting thinner—a seeming contradiction that ranks right up there with reverse polarity! Of course I have never understood why the water remains open where it does, while everything around that open lead is frozen solid. I have assumed some kind of thermal action. I guess the immediate answer to the problem is to wear my waist-high waders when I go for wood or water—and look for a text on the thermodynamics of Arctic ice.

Day 159, February 20 (Low -50, High -45, clear)

I have a very sick dog—my favorite puppy, the tank. He has the puppy illness that has been going through all the pups, but he has a complication. Along with the vomiting and diarrhea, he has either a massive hemorrhoid or something worse. I'm giving him shots for the former, but I don't know what to do for the latter. I have left a note at Mike's. Since he is a dog person, and I am not, maybe he will know what to do.

On the brighter side, I went for wood and water and didn't break through the ice. I was wearing the waders.

Day 160, February 21 (Low -51, High -28, clear)

Medical bulletin: Mike came over last night with a better dog book than the one I have been using. (*Dog Owners Veterinary Handbook*, Carlson and Giffen). Between the two of us and the text we decided that Tank was suffering from a Complete Rectal Prolapse, where a segment of intestine drops down and out of the anus. In the case of puppies this condition is usually the result of straining during diarrhea. The book said a complete rectal prolapse can be cured manually by lubricating it, and pushing it back into the anus. It further stated that to prevent a relapse a veterinarian usually puts in a temporary purse-string suture around the anus to hold it in place while healing. The only alternative to this procedure seems to be a slow and painful death, or a quick one by gunshot.

So, with Vaseline for the lubricant and crushed aspirin and

water for a local anesthetic, a sewing needle and regular white thread, we performed the whole works right here in the cabin. Actually, the "we" is misleading. Mike did it all. (I'm beginning to suspect that he is a closet renaissance man.) Tank is now on a diet of mild food; egg powder and water, mooseburger, and rice. There are still a few questions: When will the sutures come out, or when should we take them out? Will there be infection? We were hardly working in a sterile environment. To complicate matters, the intestine, while it was protruding, was badly frostbitten. What will that do now that its back inside? As of now Tank is fine. Stay tuned.

Day 161, February 22 (Low -45, High -30, light snow)

This morning Tank had relapsed. The thread had broken, or rotted away, and the intestine was once again extruding. Neither Mike nor I was willing to give up, so we went through the whole procedure again, but this time using nylon dental floss for the sutures. I'm not going to feed Tank for twenty-four hours and see whether that will stop the muscle movement which forces out the intestines.

Come on Tank!

Day 162, February 23 (Low -48, High -35, clear)

Tank didn't make it. He relapsed again and had to be shot. The alternative would have been to take him to the village and fly him from there to a vet in Fairbanks or Anchorage. If either Mike or I could have faced another round of suturing, we would have tried it again. A short life for the Tanker. *Vive le Tank.*

Day 163, February 24 (Low -47, High -38, clear)

Where did the day go? It went thusly: I got up about nine in the morning because that's when it gets light now. Cooked a light breakfast and put water on the stove for dog food. Fed the dogs about ten-thirty with commercial dog food soaked in warm water with a couple of cups of melted lard added. They get warm water for dessert. I read a few chapters of a biography of Douglas MacArthur while waiting to see whether it would warm up when the sun came up. It didn't.

I took the sled, saw and ax, and Tank's body downriver. I put

Tank in a little meadow on top of the snow so the birds can begin the recycling process. I cut down a paper birch and hauled it back. Then I crossed the river and cut a dead spruce, hauled it back and picked up drinking water on the way. Cut and split the wood and hauled it into the cabin. I made another trip downriver for spruce boughs to build a lean-to for one of the puppies.

I baked a batch of raisin, walnut, chocolate chip, oatmeal cookies while waiting for the evening meals — mine and the pups' — to cook. The walnut taste in the cookies was extremely subtle because I forgot to put any in.

Tonight, more MacArthur, and I will probably bake a chocolate cake. (Did!)

Day 164, February 25 (Low -48, High -34, clear)
Began construction of the anti-gravity, semi-pendular reading chair and leg exerciser.

Day 165, February 26 (Low -47, High -35, clear)
Primo day in the Arctic! Sunny, clear and windless.

Foxie, one of the small pups, broke through the ice today and almost drowned. When I saw she was not going to be able to extricate herself, I snaked out on my belly and snatched her from the jaws of death by the scruff of her neck. Adult sled dogs roll in the snow to dry off, but Foxie just stood there looking slightly puzzled. So I tucked her under my arm and headed for the cabin, breaking several sprint records en route. When I got there I was holding the only Arctic armadillo in captivity until I could warm Foxie up and towel off the ice.

While she was thawing out, I completed the anti-gravity, semi-pendular reading chair and leg exerciser. (Basically, it's a swing suspended from the ceiling, with a backpack frame attached for a backrest. It not only is a technological break-through, but is orthopedically sound. Five months in the planning, two hours to build.)

Day 166, February 27 (Low -53, High -35, clear)
ENNUI! TODAY! (hooray!)
Like little ships caught in the Arctic Ocean, my dentures were frozen solid in a plastic rinse glass this morning.

Day 167, February 28 (Low -40, High -2, cloudy)

Relativity. I can remember very clearly when I once thought zero degrees Fahrenheit was cold. Now it seems warm! The cold spell is over for the time being, apparently. I crossed the ice hazard today for wood but may not be able to tomorrow.

Day 168, February 29 (Low -30, High -10, cloudy)

Leap Day! I invited Mike to dinner on the eve of his departure for Nome by dogsled. He should be gone for about a month. I made a stew which began as a sort of minestrone soup and ended as mini-moose mulligatawny.

 *March*

Day 169, March 1 (Low -33, High -5, clear)

Beautiful day! It always feels better around here when I have the river all to myself, which, starting today, will be the case for most of the month of March. Why do I feel that way? It ain't natural, but it feels good so it can't be all bad.

Day 170, March 2 (Low -30, High 5, cloudy)

The first day in forty for above zero temps. It feels positively warm. I changed to a light coat, light gloves and fewer socks. It feels as if it may snow.

I'm still fighting the Protestant Work Ethic. Even up here, after cutting wood all day, I sometimes feel I should be doing something. That is a hard indoctrination to overcome, but if I don't do anything else in my life, I can at the very least accomplish that.

Day 171, March 3 (Low -20, High 15, cloudy)

The Iditarod Sled Dog Race began today. I now have two friends engaged in two of the toughest races run anywhere. John Cooper, the owner of "my" puppies, and my "next-door" neighbor, is in the Iditarod, a race from Anchorage to Nome; and Jeff King, my neighbor and co-worker at the park, is in the Yukon Quest, a race from Fairbanks to Whitehorse, Yukon Territory. Both these races can take up to two weeks or more to cover the more than a thousand miles, and just finishing is a real accomplishment for both man and dogs. This is day eight in the Yukon Quest and as of last night Jeff was in third at Dawson. It's too soon to tell about John.

Day 172, March 4 (Low 0, High 20, light snow)

Bogey, the largest pup, began eating the lean-to I had built for the two smaller pups, so I banished him to a tree by himself. These dogs are fed well, but they will still eat anything. Aside from recycling their own food three or four times, I have so far seen them eat spruce trees, paper birch, willow, plastic of all kinds, any and all parts of a dogsled, Mylar, rope, covered wire, straw, leaves, gunnysacks, foam rubber, and, in fact, any detritus of the petro-chemical industry. And that's in the semi-pristine Arctic. The mind boggles at what they would consume if turned loose in a major urban garbage dump.

Day 173, March 5 (Low -5, High 15, clear)

It was a beautiful, sunny day so I took a hike upriver with the two pups. When the weather isn't too cold to enjoy the scenery, this is really incredible country. I'm looking forward to hiking, exploring, and just sitting around watching spring happen.

Day 174, March 6 (Low 0, High 30, cloudy)

Foxie went through the ice again, and I had to belly out again to save her. So what else is new?

Day 175, March 7 (Low 5, High 30, clear)

I hiked downriver a couple of miles but was eventually stopped cold by a huge mass of overflow. It was a good thing I wasn't going anywhere. The alternative would have been to take the deep snow off the river, and that would have required snowshoes which I hadn't brought with me. A dog team would have had a real problem getting through that stuff.

Vagrant thought #148: If one were to begin reading one book a day from birth and lived to a hundred, one would still be able to read only 36,500 books in a lifetime. A good metropolitan library probably has a half-million titles. Therefore, no matter how intelligent we are, and no matter how smart we get, we are still doomed to die dumb. Socrates, you were right! (Or was that Aristotle?)

Day 176, March 8 (Low -10, High 30, clear)

Wow! Another fine day! I think I might have got a little sunburn on my face today, in contrast to a bit of frostbite only a few days ago. It will no doubt be getting cold again, but there are definitely intimations of spring.

There is a whole lot of canine-type noise outside, which reminds me, as I'm sure it was meant to, that it is about time for the dogs' dinner. It is sure nice to be able to feed them while it is still light.

Day 177, March 9 (Low 5, High 30, cloudy)

Last night, about seven-thirty, the sky was very special. To the east it was a deep, dark blue; to the west it was much lighter, with a tint of pink. Where the two colors met, directly above, floated a quarter moon, a lunar demarcation.

Relativity: A few nights ago, after the lead dog teams of the Yukon Quest race had passed through the village of Central (there is a curious contemporaneous pun in that name), the one-room building housing the town's only public telephone burned to the ground.

For the next two days — after phone service was restored — the main topic of conversation between the KJNP reporter and a lady in Central was the state of the telephone system, rather than the race. KJNP's reporting descended from that level thereafter, reaching its nadir when, during a telephonic discussion with someone in Carmacks, Yukon, the subject of the weather was interrupted briefly, and as an aside, to mention that Sonny Linder, a race contestant, "had arrived in Whitehorse at one-twenty." Nothing further was said on that subject. This was curious because Mr. Linder's arrival, since it preceded all other arrivals, made him number one, a numerical reference which in the context of racing events, is usually translated as "winner." I still don't know how, or whether, Jeff King finished.

Day 178, March 10 (Low 10, High 31, clear)

The current warm spell has apparently affected my mind. I keep getting mental images of me lolling on a beach somewhere on the subcontinent of India.

Day 179, March 11 (Low 11, High 32, cloudy)

A quick retroactive glance at this journal indicates that today is

the first day of all above-freezing temps since November 29.

I suspect I'm becoming a genuine recluse. I'm really enjoying having the river to myself, even if there are a few dogs about. There are not many places left where you can practice your primal screams without alarming the populace unduly.

Perseverance pays off: Almost every evening, just before dark, I go to a spot where I can look downriver hoping to see a moose or caribou moving along the river's edge. Tonight a moose came upriver toward me, but when he was still a long way off he apparently scented me, spooked, and tore off through the brush. Too far to shoot and too late to track.

Day 180, March 12 (Low 15, High 33, cloudy)

I tried to track last night's moose this morning, but he didn't go where I thought he would and I soon lost his tracks. So much for the ace tracker of the Arctic.

Things are getting mushy from the warmth. I'm ready for more cold.

Communication: I've begun picking up via shortwave a very weird rock station with the call letters KYOI, which apparently emanates from Saipan.

I have just spent the last half-hour at dusk watching a three-quarter moon coming up between the mountains, and listening to the silence of an Arctic evening. Ethereal!

Day 181, March 13 (Low 20, High 32, cloudy)

Some watchdogs I've got! I went out this morning and discovered moose tracks within a hundred feet of my cabin. He (or she) had been feeding on willow twigs along the river and had come right up to a spot below the cabin before turning around. I don't know why the dogs were not aware of its presence. As it is, they raise a ruckus only when I leave without taking them along, or when it's time for them to eat, or, to be more accurate, when they think it's time for them to eat.

Day 182, March 14 (Low 15, High 30, light snow)

Listening to Radio Moscow today on shortwave I learned that in the USSR there is a city of some quarter-million inhabitants, called Norilsk, that is about the same distance above the Arctic

Circle as I am here in total wilderness. Actually, at 69 degrees latitude it is a little farther north.

Listening to Radio Moscow, by the way, can be very insidious. I have to turn it off when I feel myself starting to lean left. But you never know about the after-effects. Like right now I'm feeling kind of communal. On no! Help! I'm changing! Aarrgh. . . .

Now, comrade, as I was saying. . . .

From the Homer, Alaska, version of "Trapline Chatter" on radio station KBBI: "To the Slow Boat Works, 'Is my oar done yet?' from Fast Eddy."

Day 183, March 15 (Low 20, High 25, light snow)
I washed my jeans today. They have been blood-stained, hanging frozen from a peg in the storm porch, since we skinned the moose several months ago. Like everything else around here, they were preserved perfectly by the extreme cold. I thawed them out, then rinsed them in cold water just as if they had been blood-stained earlier in the day rather than almost half a year ago.

Today was spring cleaning day as I re-arranged the cabin to put the desk/table where it would best utilize the increasing amount of daylight. It may even help to bring me and the typewriter into some sort of detente, but I doubt it.

I have had a terrible time getting radio reports on the Iditarod race. Finally, last night, I heard that John Cooper was tenth about two hundred miles from the finish. It's been a tough, slow race because of unusually warm weather. If John can hold on to tenth or somewhere in that area of finishing, I would say that's a real and very heroic accomplishment.

Day 184, March 16 (Low 15, High 20, light snow)
Always eschewing precipitous behavior, I waited until today to bake my first loaf of yeast bread in the Arctic. I finally got jaded with bannock. And besides, I have about five pounds of peanut butter to finish before summer and bannock is more for a honey-type bread-spread. (The yeast bread turned out gourmandisi-acally.)

The snow has covered all the dog detritus, thank goodness, but there is a certain retroactivity embodied in that fact which bodes ill for the future.

Day 185, March 17 (Low 5, High 15, clear)

A worthy day to wait for. Cold, crisp like good lettuce, and clear. There seems to be an increase in animal activity. Lots of tracks of moose, fox, marten; more gray jays and ravens.

I'm going to have green moose steak tonight, not as one might suppose in honor of St. Pat's Day, although that, indeed, is being celebrated this very day, but rather because the recent warm spell has temporarily put my natural freezer on the fritz.

Day 186, March 18 (Low -5, High 15, sunny)

I got back from a day of woodcutting in the bright sunshine and, feeling sort of feverish, I began mentally compiling a list of possible illnesses I might be in the process of entertaining, when it occurred to me that the malady is a common one, but not usually at this latitude. Sunburn.

Day 187, March 19 (Low -10, High 10, clear)

Heavy air traffic on the river today. In the space of about twenty minutes two small planes landed out on the river in front of the cabin. They were the second and third planes to land in the last six months. (The first was my own, last September.) Both planes were National Park Service, the pilots of which claimed to be "on business," but since no "business" was forthcoming from either, and given the pleasantness of the weather, I am led to suspect it was a severe case of joyriding. If this keeps up I'll have to put up a wind sock and hire an air traffic controller.

A few days ago I facetiously wrote about the potential danger which may derive from listening too long to Radio Moscow. I would like now to amend my remarks. There is yet another danger riding the airwaves. The threat is bifurcated, as it were. Not just Radio Moscow can be heard these days, but several religious stations are shortwaving as well, and almost nothing else. AM is apparently being solared out of existence. The insidiousness is therefore twofold, and unless guarded against, one is liable to suffer the ultimate transmogrification and become a Chris-Com!

Day 188, March 20 (Low -10, High 15, clear)

I had something very erudite to say on the subject of Language

Intimidation. It came to me as I lay in bed early this morning, arriving as many of my more intangible philosophic concepts do. But as it came it went, leaving, unlike the Cheshire Cat, not a smile but a title, and nothing more.

Thinking back on yesterday and the air raids, I'm tempted to anthropomorphize the behavior of the two youngest pups. As it happened, each of the two times a plane swooped down out of the sky and landed on the river ice, the two pups and I were in the middle of crossing it. Each time, the pups ran hell-bent for the woods and didn't show themselves again until the aircraft had left. I, on the other hand, felt compelled to hang around and act as host. The anthropomorphology comes into play in the way the pups responded to me after each plane had left. As soon as the planes were airborne the pups ventured out on the ice, presumably to see whether the huge birds had left any of my carcass lying around. At least that is what I presume from the way they greeted me each time as they saw that I was still with them, alive and well.

Day 189, March 21 (Low -15, High 0, north wind)
The snow was blowing and going today. It was the hardest north wind for a month or more. I got so excited over the meteorological situation that I decided to bake a strawberry/peach pie.

Day 190, March 22 (Low -16, High 10, clear)
On shortwave radio today, Harry Reasoner described a new word, new to me at any rate. It is "prepone," the opposite, I guess, of "postpone." The implications deriving from the potential uses of this new word are positively extraordinary. To wit: If there is something nasty that you must do, like digging out the outdoor trench toilet which is frozen solid (a personal case in point), you can *postpone* the job until spring thaw, when it would be smellier but easier. But far better would be to *prepone* the odoriferous task, which means setting it aside to do some time in the past — say two months ago, which means it's already done! Or does it? "Think about it," said Reasoner. I'm thinking, I'm thinking.

I went up to Don's cabin today and fired up his two stoves to take the chill off, since he was due back today. I did this, not out of a sense of neighborliness, but for a very selfish reason. I knew if I built the fires he wouldn't show up, and I could enjoy one more day of upper-river, recluse-style, solitude. It worked like a charm, as they used to say medievally.

Day 191, March 23 (Low -10, High 5, clear)
I have been transmitting ESP messages (the only kind possible around here) to John to please return and reclaim his puppies. I don't expect him for a week or so, but I am definitely getting puppied-out. Take Rastus, for example, who is either the most optimistic dog extant, or the dumbest. All the dogs are chained with the exception of the two youngest. The chained dogs, of course, love to be let loose to run. Rastus, however, apparently assumes that whenever I touch him, even to feed or pet him, I am undoing his chain. Accordingly, he immediately accelerates to about one-hundred-twenty mph and heads in a straight trajectory out of the dog yard. After about ten feet he hits the end of the still-fastened chain, becomes airborne, performs a one-hundred-eighty-degree reverse half-gainer, and crashes to earth on his back. There is a relatively prominent indentation in the snow where he usually lands. A circumstance that has occurred about fifty times.

Day 192, March 24 (Low -15, High 5, clear)
I went up to John's today to get some fish oil for the dogs. It's a cold-weather supplement, the same as the lard which I have almost run out of. There was lots of evidence of overflow from last week's warm spell, but all frozen solid now. It was the first time Foxie and Bunnock, the two small pups, had been on glare ice. They looked like first-time roller skaters, but they learned quickly.
Don returned today and I finally learned how John did in the Iditarod. Ninth! Very good, and Don said that $3,200 went along with that finish. In a race as tough as the Iditarod, just to finish is a victory. This year, about one-third of the sixty-eight contestants scratched during the race, and some of them finished several days after the winner had crossed the finish line.

Day 193, March 25 (Low -14, High 10, clear)
While building a fire this morning, I became aware that the anticipation of warmth has become a real pleasure. The fact that I have to create it adds a dimension that a thermostat would kill.

Day 194, March 26 (Low -20, High 5, clear)

I am going to set an upper-river baking record by the end of the day. I have already produced four dozen chocolate chip cookies; bread dough is rising at this writing; and unless plans change, I shall bake a chocolate/banana pie this evening. Then I'm going to sit back and eat the whole works. Fat City!

Day 195, March 27 (Low 0, High 15, snow)

About four inches of snow fell last night, covering, once again, an estimated five tons of doggie-do. Come spring, look out!

Speaking of those animals, having already been guilty of anthropomorphizing the two little pups, I may as well do the older ones. So, here are a few dog portraits: Moon, sometimes called "Moon Over Miami," or "Moonlight Sonata," which confuses the hell out of the dog, but saves me from boredom. Moon is an exact canine clone of the blond-haired kid in the "Our Gang" movies, even down to the voice. Like the kid, Moon has a speech impediment, and can bark only in a kind of raspy whisper. Again like the kid, Moon looks sort of albino-ish. You set a baseball cap at a crooked angle on Moon's head, and he could be in the movies!

Rastus is a chunky little dog who likes to sit on top of his lean-to like a bird. (Saying that a dog acts birdlike is not anthropomorphizing. I don't know what it is.) Anyway, as a consequence of his birdy behavior the Rastus domicile is now a pile of sticks and a crumpled wad of .06 mil plastic. I repaired it a half-dozen times. No more. Rastus likes to bark, particularly around mealtime, but he will not bark if I am pointing my finger at him, even from quite a distance, so we have this game. I will point at him, whereupon he desists from barking. Then when I turn to walk away, he immediately resumes barking. But every once in awhile instead of turning one-hundred-eighty degrees, I do a three-hundred-sixty and end up pointing at him again. Meanwhile, Rastus has been inhaling huge volumes of air in preparation for his next series of barks, but now he is faced with that same accusing finger and there ensues in rapid succession over his face, evidence of chagrin, perplexity, and finally, downright discomfort as he attempts to discover a socially acceptable method of expelling all that air.

Akla is a jerk. The classic prototype of the cowardly bully. A sand-kicker. But worse, Akla is a wheamer. The wheam occupies the auditory territory somewhere between a whine and a scream. Akla has perfected the wheam to heights other dogs only dream of. The loose skin along the sides of his mouth quiver and vibrate, and an unholy sound issues forth. Akla wheams for food, and for petting; Akla wheams when his siblings are petted; and he wheams whenever he wants to be turned loose, which is whenever I leave the cabin. Akla will wheam at the drop of a snowflake. The sound of wheaming is unamusing. As an object lesson Akla should be taken out and shot in mid-wheam.

Robin, the lone female of the litter of four, must have excess body heat, along with a penchant for sleeping in only one spot. All of the dogs form shallow, sunken circles three or four inches deep where they curl up and sleep in the frozen snow. Robin's siblings have two or three of these where they alternate as the whim takes them. Robin has only one, and it is at present about a foot-and-a-half deep and still sinking.

Day 196, March 28 (Low 0, High 29, north wind)

My sleep habits are following the daylight hours. This morning I awoke and got up about seven-thirty, after bedding down around midnight. That is a far cry from midwinter, when I was sleeping at least twelve hours each night. There are about fourteen hours of daylight now. By the time I head out in late May there will be twenty plus.

Day 197, March 29 (Low 5, High 20, north wind)

I shaved for the first time in six months, and if one were to look closely, one could perhaps even see the difference between before and after. But not much. Big deal.

Day 198, March 30 (Low 0, High 20, windy)

Whatever happened to the BFCs? (And the squirrels, for that matter.) I haven't heard or seen a BFC in the cabin for weeks. The squirrels are subdued because of the puppy prevalence, but I haven't even seen one for several days. Maybe they are all rehearsing for the upcoming Rites of Spring.

Yesterday it blew hard again, at a guess thirty to forty mph, maybe more. Around the cabin it doesn't matter, but away from it those winds could be a problem.

Last evening at dusk I went out into the wind shadow made by the point in front of the cabin. Downriver the wind was causing dust devils made from snow to dance across the overflow. And the wind was eddying around the point just as the river has and will again when it flows.

Day 199, March 31 (Low 0, High 30, cloudy)

I have had the pups for more than a month now since John went off to the Iditarod wars. It has caused me to become quite religious. I pray every day. It is a simple but fervent little prayer. It is, "COME HOME JOHN!"

 *April*

Day 200, April 1 (Low 25, High 40, clear)

The upper river was hit with a massive attack of warmth today. The snow is getting wet and mushy. Woodcutting was a sweat! More cold please.

As if in answer to my query of a day or so ago, the squirrels and BFCs have returned. Yesterday the squirrels were scolding the puppies, the gray jays and one another. This morning I awoke to find a BFC standing innocently in my chocolate pie, staring at me from across the room. (There are very few creatures that can maintain an innocent attitude while standing in chocolate pie. As it happens, members of the BFC are able to do this. No one, to my knowledge, knows why.) Had the culprit been just a tad closer, I would have made Creme de Cacao out of the bugger.

Day 201, April 2 (Low 30, High 40, light snow)

This was a down day. Don't know why. Didn't do anything. Didn't want to. Still don't.

Day 202, April 3 (Low 15, High 20, snow)

This started out to be another down day, but was rescued by the advent of four inches of new snow, and a baking adventure involving spicy hermit cookies and lemon pie. It was further enlightened with the discovery of an ancient (pre-me, anyway) bag of semisweet chocolate chips, a condiment included on the endangered species list here.

Day 203, April 4 (Low 5, High 20, clear)

I didn't know what to write tonight until a few minutes ago.

Now I do. It's about a miracle. One that could be the basis for the founding of a new religion, albeit a canine one, and I don't know how that would go over with the masses. (No pun intended, RCs.) It happened thusly: Looking at this blank paper, my thoughts were interrupted by a flurry of dog barks, and then I noticed Akla was running loose. Akla, Moon, Rastus and Robin are all chained close together but only Moon's and Akla's chains overlap. The chains are affixed to the collars by a common, spring-loaded gate hook similar to what old-fashioned janitors carry their key rings on, and the same as virtually all San Francisco gays wear hooked to their jeans belt loops as part of their regular uniforms. When I went out to see how Akla had got loose, I found Moon chained between two chains, his own, and Akla's! Now, at the moment, as far as I know, there is no human being other than myself any-where near here, so the two dogs, in wrestling or whatever, contrived to unhook the spring-loaded hook from Akla's collar and re-hook it on Moon's. I dunno, folks, I welcome a little break in the routine, but this borders on the weird, flaky, and Arctic-strange.

Day 204, April 5 (Low 5, High 20, clear)

Quality comment: Having just finished reading a Zane Grey paperback entitled *The Last Ranger*, I'm reminded once again that publishers apparently don't bother to read these old books before they are reprinted. The theory probably is that they were proven sellers, so who needs to read them? This particular book has no "Ranger," in it, last, first, or otherwise. The cover has an illustra-tion of a big, strapping cowboy complete with six-gun, Stetson, cowboy boots and chaps, denim jacket, and a repeating rifle hanging from the end of his arm. All very appropriate, you might say, for a Zane Grey book. But, had the publishers bothered to read it, they would have discovered that it took place in the 1750s, in the Eastern U.S., a time and place when neither the six-gun nor repeating rifle had yet been invented and cowboy dress was unknown. There was a time (wasn't there?) when that sort of thing was important.

Day 205, April 6 (Low -5, High 15, clear)

Little things made big: Bogey has a bone to chew. He's had it ever since I've known him. Maybe he brought it with him. I don't know. Twice a day Bogey remembers that he *used* to have a bone and starts whining for it, because twice a day Bogey forgets to guard the bone and either Foxie or Bunnock, who are unchained, steals it. They take it just beyond the length of Bogey's chain, where they lick away at it because it's too big for their young teeth. Twice a day I return the bone to Bogey with the admonishment that *this* is the *last* time I will come to the assistance of such a dumb dog. Twice a day I go back on my word.

Day 206, April 7 (Low -15, High 0, clear)
  Specious speculation: The BBC announced this morning that the currently spaceborne shuttle is carrying, among other things, some thirty million tomato pips which will be left in space for ten months before being returned to earth and distributed to American schoolchildren, who will plant them. The purpose of the project, said the BBC, is to determine whether the long exposure to cosmic radiation will result in any adverse affects. Ominously, the usually grammatically precise BBC did not specify whether the effects, if any, referred to the tomato pips or the schoolchildren.

Day 207, April 8 (Low -20, High -10, clear)
  The anti-gravity, semi-pendular, reading-chair and leg-exerciser, mentioned earlier, is complete, and in its completeness functions as an unintended personality test. This is not exactly Grand Central Station, so only two persons, other than myself, have had occasion to see the A-G S-P R-C and L-E in its final glory. And it is glorious (or at least peculiar). Made from yarn, steel cable, bits of caribou fur, an old back-pack frame, foam rubber, and two pieces of rag, it has a certain majesty as it hangs expectantly from the ridgepole, waiting, as it were, for something to happen. Because it is affixed to the ridgepole it has a somewhat dominant position in a twelve-by-fourteen-foot cabin. One might even call it overwhelming. The first person to view the completed A-G etcetera was Don, the occasional occupant of the upriver cabin. After being absent for more than a month, Don came to visit, looked around the cabin, and said, "I see you have made some changes." He never mentioned nor looked at the A-G etc.

again during the remainder of the evening. The second viewee
was also a Don, a friend of and visitor to the earlier Don, from the
village. He called on me last evening, making what I presume was
to him an obligatory neighborly visit, since we hadn't met before.
We had a nice chat, covering a wide variety of subjects, not
including the A-G etc. Don took a seat by the window, and as far
as I could tell, never saw the A-G etc. even though it requires a
sidling maneuver around the A-G etc. to get from the door to the
window seat and vice versa. These rather bizarre happenings
have led me to toy with the idea that the A-G etc. may be invisible
to everyone but me. Stranger things, I'm sure, have happened in
the Arctic.

Day 208, April 9 (Low -30, High -10)
    As already noted the shortwave radio waves carry a wonderful
mixture of Communism and Christianity. Today, the Christian
transmitters are stronger. Perhaps He is helping them. In any
case, the word for the day is "hold tightly to the slippery spar of
life." I believe this was the tail-end (tale end?) of a parable
describing the sinking of the *Lusitania* in frigid northern waters.
But I missed all that.

Day 209, April 10 (Low -30, High -10, clear)
    Dog day in the Arctic. Actually, it's a no-dog day because John
returned last night and will pick up the pups today. The squirrels,
birds and BFCs will be pleased.
    Weather-wise, today was a day and a half.
    Word power: According to Solzhenitsyn, the word *podkulachnik*
seemed to be quite a logical term in his youth. It was defined as an
accomplice of a kulak, the latter being anyone who hired workers.
So, although the word appeared harmless, being called that *after*
the revolution could get you banished to the Gulag for life.

Day 210, April ?? (Low -15, High 10, clear)
    I don't know if this has happened to other chroniclers, but I
seem to have misplaced a day. Or else it simply didn't happen,
which seems unlikely. Yesterday was April 10. Today is April 12.
Therefore. . . .
    Forget all the above. I was listening to Radio Moscow and

forgot that there is an intervening International Date Line. It's the eleventh.

Day 211, April 12 (Low -30, High -10, clear)

Today is the anniversary of the insertion of the first man into space. Unfortunately he was Russian, so it doesn't count.

From the last entry the reader may sense that this ship is in danger of losing its rudder. Based on the possible disintegration of the writer, and the hazards of travel during breakup — not enough snow for dogs, not enough unfrozen water for boats, and too much standing water for hiking — I have decided to leave about a month from now, providing some flexibility for meteorological piquancies.

Day 212, April 13 (Low -25, High 10, clear)

I had almost forgotten what a joy climbing can be. Today I climbed a ridge, wearing snowshoes, in preparation for climbing up to a shelf high above the river. A shelf I have been eyeballing greedily all winter. Today I was just building a trail partway up, but even a gain in elevation of only a few hundred feet opened a great, mountainous panorama. It was very tiring in the deep, drifted snow, but tomorrow the trail will be packed and set-up as far as I went, and the rest of the way to the shelf should be easy. The shelf, itself, is about a thousand to fifteen hundred feet above the river and should offer a tremendous view.

Day 213, April 14 (Low -10, High 10, snow)

Too snowy to climb, so I took the back trail upriver instead. I saw a moose browsing on willow but never got very close to it.

Day 214, April 15 (Low 0, High 10, light snow)

Seven months of Arctic winter as of today. In that time I have had human interaction with fewer than ten people. It would be nice to find a place where it wasn't so crowded. I'm joking, of course, but I will say this: The happiest I've been up here is when I have been completely alone.

Errant thought: The nicest outhouse in North America is located in the Sonora Desert at Organ Pipe Cactus National Monument in southwest Arizona. It is located in a primitive campground, and if you prop the door open the view looks south into Mexico over the tops of cholla, saguaro, organ pipe, and assorted other cacti.

Day 215, April 16 (Low -10, High 0, light snow)
Lying in bed this morning, reading, I was suddenly engulfed with a powerful premonition that indicated if I put on my snow-shoes, grabbed my rifle, and headed for John's on the back trail, the present meat shortage would be solved by a moose, who would step out in front of me and pose. I did, but the moose didn't. So much for powerful premonitions.

Day 216, April 17 (Low -20, High -5, light snow)
I'm making a shopping list! John and I are going to two Eskimo villages by dogsled tomorrow. As a reward for my taking care of the pups John suggested that we make the trip because he needs fuel supplies, but the real reason we're going is to attend a poetry reading by Gary Snyder. That was such a suitably flaky reason for making a forty-mile dogsled trip in subzero weather that there was no way I could or would refuse. I met Gary back in the late '60s and it will be nice to see him again. Having spent the last seven months in Eskimo country without meeting any Eskimos, I guess its time to rectify that too.

Day 217, 218 & 219, April 18, 19, 20 (Low -10, High 0, clear)
A splendid three days! A dogsled trip of forty-plus miles over varied, pristine snowscape to the little Eskimo village of Kobuk, a collection of old and new abodes on the banks of the Kobuk River. There to attend a poetry reading by famed poet and philosopher Gary Snyder. (In 1960, he and Allen Ginsberg, walk-ing the streets of Kathmandu wherein the former said to the latter, "Allen, the hippies are going to love this place!" They did, too well to suit the Nepalese.) A poetry reading, as it turned out, attended by only two persons, who had traveled forty miles by dogsled over three river valleys and across various mountain passes to be present. Snyder was impressed by the calibre of his audience, if not by its numbers.
Next day to Shungnak, another Eskimo village, about ten miles down the Kobuk, a distance I drove with five dogs pulling an

©Dassow 87

Iditarod racing sled, the very one that brought John to his ninth place finish. I "finished" my ten-mile run to Shungnak without embarassing John, myself or the dogs.

A birthday party that night was attended by a half-dozen local teachers. We consumed a fine meal of salad, lasagne, poroshkis, home brew and three kinds of ice cream. Our hosts, Hans and Bonnie, have an outdoor privy located on the side of a steep bank which is reached by climbing a permanently anchored rope, with a rappel down afterward.

Adding one dog to my team the following day, I drove the Iditarod sled twenty miles back until we hit windblown snow and the larger sled loaded with fuel refused to track properly. So we hooked the two sleds together, combined the two dog teams, and John guided the big sled with a gee pole.

We arrived home around nine in the evening with plenty of light to spare. I had such a good time I decided to stay through breakup for sure, even if it means cutting it close in getting back to work on time.

Day 220, April 21 (Low 10, High 30, north wind)

Very high north winds all day. More snow is being blown around my cabin than at any time during the winter. It may be blowing out winter and ushering in spring. Breakup, I'm told, can happen unbelievably fast, so, I'm poised here waiting for it to happen.

Two harbingers of spring: snow buntings are back; also, on our return from Shungnak I noticed some of the willows were displaying new catkins!

Day 221, April 22 (Low 10, High 20, clear)

I spent part of the day digging out from the windblown snow. The trail to the privy trench was under about three feet of drifts.

Lots of sunshine, but I'm still recovering from the three-day trip and the outdoors does not beckon so fetchingly at the moment.

Day 222, April 23 (Low -5, High 20, cloudy)

I hiked about five miles today. The wind dropped and switched from north to south. John is going to begin ferrying supplies from the village by dogsled before breakup, and as a consequence I have inherited another wounded dog. This one has a sore foot.

Day 223, April 24 (Low 0, High 10, light snow)
Things are assuming serious proportions in discussing how to exit this place sometime in the next month. Don and I have talked of hiking out some forty miles to the village. Another plan is to hike to Doug and Christy's and take a canoe cached there last fall (the same canoe I used to haul my supplies across the river on September 15). But that's out. The owner let us know via KJNP last night that the canoe should remain upriver. The other alternatives are to go out by dogsled before breakup (too early) or by boat after breakup (maybe too late). We'll see. Suspense is healthy.

Day 224, April 25 (Low 0, High 15, light snow)
Waffling: I guess I'm going to leave as I arrived — waffling. I waffled most of last summer trying to decide whether or not to come up here. Now I'm waffling on whether to leave early or late. A few minutes ago I waffled over whether or not to write about waffling.

Day 225, April 26 (Low 5, High 20, sunny)
I found *my* piece of land today. More than a thousand feet above the river on a narrow shelf that juts out from the mountain like the bow of a ship, this is the place I had planned to climb up to more than a week ago. I've been looking at it all winter and today I finally climbed up there. The view is just incredible, up or down the valley. It's totally isolated. More than likely there is no water there in the summer. Nobody in his right mind would want such an isolated piece of property, given the difficulty of hauling supplies up to it. Except maybe me. If the State ever opens up this country for land disposal again, I'd stake it and prove it out in a flash.

Day 226, April 27 (Low 5, High 31, sunny)
The solar flares have fled! Or something. For the last three days I have had zero radio reception. No AM except when it is dark, which it isn't much anymore. Not even any shortwave. Zilch. None. *Nada.* Tonight, though, at six, I turned on the Voice Of America Jazz Hour expecting the usual nothing, and there it was,

loud and clear. Well, the saints preserve us! Or at least, go marchin' in.

Time is getting short. I've still got to finish the roof I started last September, if it ever thaws. And I want to tan the bear hide. I was going to type this journal before leaving, but I have rationalized a reason not to: I'll send the typewriter out with John on his last dogsled trip to the village so I won't have to carry it.

Day 227, April 28 (Low 20, High 32, snow)

Martens are something else! I have been interacting (I guess that is the correct term) with a marten all morning. This particular creature, like the one I encountered last fall, is unafraid. It's about half the size of a house cat (all that fur is misleading). I had the feeling it was going to attack me on more than one occasion. First, I ran it out of the storm porch where it had crawled through an incredibly narrow crack and was eating my butter. It left, but kept returning. Finally, I chased it up a tree, where it climbed just out of reach, turned, and growled at me. I was trying to frighten it off before it dug through the snow on the roof and put holes in the plastic. At last I broke off the engagement to cross the river for water. When I returned it was gone, but not for long, I'll wager.

It snowed at least half a foot today.

Day 228, April 29 (Low 20, High 32, snow)

A foot of new snow in the last two days! Strange. I was all ready to exit the Arctic, but have now decided to stay until the last dog dies. (Now that I think about it, that's an unfortunate phrase to use in mushing country.) I'll stay until about May 22 and walk out to the village if the river ice is still solid. In the meantime, I'll relax and enjoy spring, assuming it's coming this year.

Day 229, April 30 (Low 32, High 32, snow)

Still snowing! About a foot and a half, maybe even two, has fallen in the past three days. The snow is very wet, not at all like the dry snow of winter. It would be almost impossible to travel in this stuff. The babiche on snowshoes would clog up and weigh tons. The dogs would sink in to their chests. A mess, but very pretty. I'm glad I'm not traveling.

The first junco of spring was sighted on the last day of April.

May

Day 230, May 1 (Low 15, High 24, cloudy)

To the untrained eye — both of my eyes fall into that category — the land hereabouts hardly seems on the verge of breakup. There is more snow on the ground, at greater depth, than at any time during the winter. The smaller spruce trees are shattering midway down their trunks and breaking in half from the unbearable loads of snow. The river is still, a vast, sleeping serpent lying prostrate across the countryside. The sky is gray and unpromising. There is no evidence of the sun. Happy May Day to one and all!

Belay all the above! The sun just came out. The snow is cascading off the trees like lumps of confetti. And everything is gorgeous.

Earlier today two moose — the plural and singular for all members of the deer family are the same — a cow and yearling calf, walked by my window not more than ten feet away. While I was reading at my window bench, I heard the crunching of snow and suddenly there they were. I suppose, in true Arctic spirit, I should have killed one, as meat for John's and Mike's dogs, but I didn't.

Day 231, May 2 (Low 0, High 15, cloudy)

Hold it Mack, winter's back!

Day 232, May 3 (Low -5, High 15, clear)

This cold weather (when it's supposed to be warm) is messing up my schedule. I had set aside this month for aesthetics: bird-watching, river-listening, flower-feeling, and so forth, not including work. I had, I thought, cut enough wood to last, with about a half-cord to leave for the next tenant (which is a half-cord more than was here when I came). So, today I did a little timber cruising across the river, and tomorrow I'll cut and haul for the first time in several weeks.

Day 233, May 4 (Low 0, High 20, snow)
The river is groaning occasionally, either because of the added weight of recently fallen snow or because it is experiencing early signs of breakup. But winter is reluctant to give up its hold on the land. (Mike says the Natives in the village are suggesting breakup may not happen this year until June.)

John came by and said if I'm going to walk out I should do it within the next week. Otherwise it may be impossible to get out by the twenty-eighth. What to do? It is semi-dilemmic. It all depends on the weather, and it is axiomatic that anyone who depends on Arctic weather is crazy.

I took out my frustrations today by massacring a dead tree, cutting and slashing among the falling snowflakes with a startling display of sylvan pillage and plunder.

Day 234, May 5 (Low 0, High 22, clear)
The last of the "Across The River And Into The Trees" wood-chopping expeditions took place today. As I pulled the loaded sled across the ice where I have broken through several times, I thanked the Ice Gods for allowing this last safe passage of the winter.

At the exact moment I spoke this benediction the rope I was towing the sled with parted, leaving me safe on the near side and the sled sitting ominously on the thinnest, most treacherous span of ice. Well! A lesser man would have left the sled and its load of wood right where it was until breakup, when it would have joined the ice on its journey to the Bering Sea. Not I. Lustily singing the theme song from Doctor Zhivago, "Somewhere my love...." and pretending unawareness of the Ice Gods' little joke, I strode resolutely out onto the ice (It is possible to stride resolutely on snowshoes, but it is darn difficult.), retied the parted knot, and re-strode off again, safely. The Ice Gods did not strike, I thought smugly, but then I thought, winter isn't over yet.

Day 235, May 6 (Low 28, High 38, cloudy)

First day above freezing in more than a month. Could this be a harbinger? If so, of what?

Day 236, May 7 (Low 28, High 36, snow)

Comparison: From Mike's journal of last year, the last two weeks of April were above freezing. The river went out on May twelfth. By this time Mike was working in his shorts! Spring is late this year but today the world is melting, so this may be the beginning. Mike and I are pulling for a cataclysmic breakup—a month's worth in two or three days. A Velikovskian Spring! Assuming Mike and I go downriver by boat and dogsled by the twenty-sixth, a whole lot of changes have to take place very soon: First and foremost, the breakup of the river. Then we will have to cross the huge overflow area by sled because it won't have broken loose by then. This is the area where, at last report, only the top foot of Mike's fish-camp tent was showing above the ice. The tent was at least ten feet above river level last fall, which translates to about a twenty-foot thick block of ice covering several square miles.

Day 237, May 8 (Low 32, High 38, cloudy)

The snow is melting and compacting. With assistance from me and my shovel, most of the snow is gone from the roof, an anti-leak precaution. In past years, I'm told, this cabin has flooded because, without heat, the earth is frozen beneath the flooring and there is nowhere for the snow-melt to go. John says he has seen four or five inches of water in the cabin in springtime. I have a bucket ready to bale just in case the winter-long warmth from my fires has not kept the below-the-floor area unfrozen.

The river is showing more signs of overflow but, so far, there are no open areas of water near here. The ice has caved in in places up near John's cabin. Don left for the village last night after we consumed four quarts of ice cream at Mike's. He may have waited too long for good hiking. His parting words were "See you below the circle!" Sheesh! A few months in the Arctic and he's talking like a veteran pole explorer!

Day 238, May 9 (Low 32, High 34, cloudy)

Coming back from a trip to Mike's, as I entered the trees near my cabin, I heard what sounded like about a hundred birds singing. A crescendo of crossbills? A jubilation of juncos? A benediction of buntings? A phantasmagoria of fox sparrows? I don't know, but it sure was pretty.

We need sun or rain. Days like today do not move us much closer to breakup.

Day 239, May 10 (Low 28, High 38, cloudy)
About five inches of snow fell last night and this morning. Unless something drastic happens weatherwise, I'm going to be using foot-power to get out of here. Twelve days from now will be Decision Day.

Day 240, May 11 (Low 5, High 22, clear)
I'm helping Mike build his workshop while waiting for something to happen with the winter/spring season. Nothing is melting today, even in the sun, which was out for awhile. By late afternoon it snowed again. So what else is new?

Day 241, May 12 (Low 15, High 34, snow)
Overheard on radio station KJNP: "For the past half-hour you have been listening to 'The Hour of Decision.' " Is that an example of time compression, or what?

Another three or four inches of snow last night.

Day 242, May 13 (Low 30, High 40, light snow)
Big Day! Birds! Within about a twenty-minute period Mike and I saw the first: rusty blackbird, varied thrush, snipe, and high overhead, a vee of geese heading north.

We took a trip to John's by dogsled, which may be the last by that mode this year. Spring is definitely here! Even though the temperature dropped to below freezing last night it reached forty during the day. Coming back from John's at two in the morning it was still light and a full moon made the trip transcendental.

Day 243, May 14 (Low 20, High 45, clear)
Avalanches on both sides of the valley sound like thunder as the melting snow can no longer cling to the steep mountain slopes. Another sign of breakup: Mike saw two mew gulls today. They

©LDassow87

and yesterday's geese will look long, hard, and without success for open water in the Arctic.

Day 244, May 15 (Low 20, High 45, clear)
Indecision reigns! I cannot decide when to leave. If the present weather pattern holds it is possible to go on the snow from about midnight until nine or ten in the morning because it is frozen. During the daytime the snow turns to mush and it is about three to four feet deep. There is enough light to travel any time, but I don't want to leave yet!

But if it stops freezing at night, any travel before a lot more snow melts is virtually impossible. It appears now that boating out of here and getting to the park by June 1 are incompatible goals. So, do I go now or wait until the last, hoping the snow will melt? Therein lies the puzzle. The hell with it. I think I'll wait. But, maybe I won't. On the other hand. . . .

Day 245, May 16 (Low 35, High 60, clear)
Very warm today. The first time in a long time it didn't freeze at night. So much for walking out at night. Avalanches crashed down all day today on both sides of the valley. It sounded like an artillery battle being waged, with the still-frozen river as the prize. There is running overflow out in front of the cabin as of this afternoon, so trips to get water are almost as easy as turning on a faucet. Two new birds today, a mew gull and a sandhill crane, both high overhead.

Day 246, May 17 (Low 35, High 58, clear)
Water is moving *on* the river. It is flowing over the ice, so breakup is not officially here, but it almost exactly replicates the shape of the river as it was just before freeze-up last fall. Two more new birds: a waxwing and an unknown large bird, probably an owl or hawk, that flew out of sight too quickly for me to identify it. *Mucho* sunshine, about twenty hours a day!

Day 247, May 18 (Low 35, High 60, clear)
The river is changing by the hour. It now looks very much as it did on the day I landed here, except that the bars are snow and ice instead of gravel, and the river is glacial-green rather than blue. It

is now flowing full force above the ice, and the sound of its passage will be a lullabye tonight.

Bird watch: robin, yellow legs, tree swallow, song sparrow.

Nine p.m.: I just checked on the river again. The transformation is truly astounding. It opens up a new channel about every hour, it seems, channels I had forgotten existed last fall. Watching the river come to life again would be worth wintering here, even if nothing else had happened.

Day 248, May 19 (Low 35, High 50, clear)

The river is still breaking up. Tonight or tomorrow a big mass of ice should come down and that will be official breakup for this segment of the river. It is happening fast. A goose just flew upriver about three feet off the water, honking wildly.

For the last two weeks I have been helping Mike build his log workshop. We have been peeling logs and hoisting them into place for fourteen straight days! So, tomorrow we're going to take a day off and watch the river. That will be nice.

Day 249, May 20 (Low 30, High 50, cloudy)

Mike and I did, indeed, take the day off, hoping to see the river breakup. Not yet. I baked cookies, apple pie and bread. I made a batch of spaghetti sauce with moose meat. I also finally completed the roofing job begun last fall. I chopped a bunch of wood, made some snow ice cream to go with the pie, and waited in vain for the parade of ice to begin. Still waiting. . . .

While I was waiting I created a viewing nest from which to watch the river, both up and down. It's a lovely spot covered with moss, a spruce tree to lean against, on a point above the river which is perfect for breakup watching and other riverine activities.

Day 250, May 21 (Low 32, High 45, cloudy)

Purple mountain saxifrage is blooming on the viewpoint, the first flower of spring!

The river appears to be jamming up with huge blocks of ice about half a mile above and below my cabin. It should go tonight or tomorrow.

Mike said he will go out on the twenty-eighth reaching the

village, we hope, on the twenty-ninth. That should get me to Denali on the first.

Bird watch: Arctic tern.

Day 251, May 22 (Low 30, High 40, cloudy)

I am now engaged in one of the world's strangest commutes as I wend my way to work at Mike's workshop. First, I don a pair of chest-high waders over long johns, stuff my pants, socks and shoes into a day-pack, then put on showshoes because the snow will no longer support my weight, even on the winter-packed trails. Stumbling off through the wet snow, I soon come to what was a meadow but is now a waist-deep, slow-moving creek about fifty yards wide. Thus the waders. (The dry pants, socks and shoes are carried rather than worn because the waders have sprung irreparable leaks.) Crossing the stream holding 1) the day-pack, 2) my rifle, 3) the snowshoes, and praying I don't stumble, I stagger across, re-don the snowshoes and, sounding a bit like an old washing machine, slosh onward to Mike's, hoping my feet don't freeze. On arrival I remove the now-wet long johns and socks, hang them up to dry, put on dry pants, socks and underwear, and am ready for another day of log-raising. At the end of the day the entire process is reversed. Still, it beats a New Jersey-Manhattan commute by quite a wide margin.

The river has risen as I write, but still no breakup.

Post midnight: Large chunks of ice are going down now, but still no extravaganza.

Mike is waffling about when he is leaving. The pendulum has swung back to walking out.

Day 252, May 23 (Low 35, High 53, clear)

All bets are temporarily deferred. As of now the river is not boatable (too much ice). The land is not walkable (too much mucky snow and run-off). The air is flyable (but not landable). If I don't get out of here by June 1, I may be unemployable. Morable about this later.

Day 253, May 24 (Low 32, High 55, clear)

Mike and I hiked up to John's. Part of the way was tough walking through patches of deep snow and heavy growths of alder. It was good going on the river bars, where huge chunks of ice were stranded like beached whales.

John says breakup happened at his place on the twentieth. Very dramatic. The ice jam above my place went by his cabin like an explosion. Along my stretch of river, breakup went by like a ghost.

Both John and Mike are experiencing the *manana* syndrome with regard to departure times. If I wait to go out with either of them, there is no telling when that will happen. So I'm walking out, starting Sunday, May 27. Maybe Mike will give me a lift by boat part way. Or maybe he won't.

Day 254, May 25 (Low 32, High 46, cloudy)

As I came back from John's at two this morning, there was still alpenglow on the mountaintops. The last stage of melt of the huge shore-bound ice blocks is something called ice candles. These are long, finger-thick rods of ice that form layer upon layer, and fall to the ground with a lovely musical sound when they are disturbed. We saw several moose on the way back.

Today we launched Mike's boat and gave it a brief test run.

Day 255, May 26 (Low 35, High 36, snow)

Pack, pack, pack. Snow, snow, snow.

Day 256, May 27 (Low 30, High 40, snow)

Today I performed the ultimate waffle. I decided not to try walking out. After emptying the cabin into the food cache and filling my pack with needed items, I realized that the pack was too heavy for me to safely travel over snow and ice. I hate to admit that my back is a problem, but I can't chance hiking out and have it stop working somewhere out in the Arctic boonies. So, I told Mike I would wait and go out with him, and I asked him as a favor to me to try to go out by the thirty-first so I can at least call Denali on the day I'm supposed to be there.

 *June*

Day 257 to Day 261, May 28 to June 1 (Temps 30 to 50, sunny)

The following is a five-day chronicle of an attempt to solo out of here to civilization. It was an unmitigated, dyed-in-the-wool, genuine, four-square failure. I am writing this back at my cabin on June 1, having staggered back about noon.

This wilderness version of the Hindenberg-Dien Bien Phu-Krakatoa disasters began on the late afternoon of the twenty-seventh, when Mike checked the river and declared that he couldn't leave before June 3. With the Protestant Work Ethic embroiling my pancreas and other organs, I reluctantly, very reluctantly, concluded that I should walk out. Actually, the plan was to walk downriver fifteen miles in two days, borrow a kayak from Doug and Christy, and paddle the twenty-five miles to the village. This would have put me in the village on the thirtieth and Denali Park on the first. To put it bluntly, I was scared to death (close to accurate as it turned out) by the whole enterprise, but fueled by the rightious PWE, I felt I must give it a try.

I started off on the wrong foot, figuratively if not literally, by over-packing. When I finished packing the pack weighed between sixty and seventy pounds, considerably heavier than any pack I had carried before. I thought it was *all* essential. (Two days out, I dumped about fifteen pounds of it, mostly clothes.)

Walking along an Arctic river during breakup is to encounter a whole world of strangeness. Huge blocks of ice sitting far from the river's normal banks. Immense fields of overflow ice, great to walk on if you can get to it, as I was to discover with much frustration later. Streams that *leave* the river rather than enter it, a phenomenon heretofore not encountered by me. Weird channels of water that seem to appear and disappear at their own will. The river ebbing and flowing by the minute, carrying blocks of ice downstream to pile up in huge dams, and scouring the banks of too-close trees as they went. This was how Dante would describe an Arctic Purgatory, perhaps.

Through this landscape came the hero, worried, burdened, but so far undaunted. The first day I made only six miles, forced by the river most of the time to walk through dense, boggy, hummocky spruce forest following, it seemed at times, only moments behind an unseen moose whose tracks were still filling with water or slowly crumbling along the edges. It was tense and exhausting. For most of the next five days I was in a condition of barely suppressed panic, an energy waster of a high order. When I reached six-mile ridge I was stopped cold by waist-deep snow with a thick, hard crust on it, but not hard enough to support my weight. It was agonizing to take two steps on top, then plunge through thigh-deep on the third. It was impossible to walk through, or on, with a heavy pack. I set up camp and decided to wait until about two in the morning when I hoped the freezing temperature would make it passable. It didn't. The next morning I split my pack into two carries and climbed directly over the top of the ridge to where the sun had melted the snow on the tundra. I remembered that last October Mike and I had taken a dogsled trail up there which eventually led back to the river farther downstream, where I could see overflow ice for easy walking. This consumed much of that morning, but eventually I was on my way again.

About a mile farther along I encountered a curious phenome-non mentioned earlier — a stream that flowed *out* of the river, a reverse tributary, as it were, a little too deep and fast to cross. I decided to follow it, expecting it to rejoin the main river up ahead somewhere. It did eventually, but only after winding endlessly through spruce forests punctuated periodically by overflow ice that seemed like the remnants of the last Ice Age in this otherwise placid forest. When the stream rejoined the river, I was on the wrong, or upstream side of it. The only solution to this, other than backtracking several miles, was to cross over an ice bridge about fifteen feet above the stream, spanning about thirty feet and appearing to be about six inches thick at its thinnest. I made it across, tiptoeing all the way, but then decided I was a damn fool to take such a risk. It could have ended with a broken leg, or me helplessly pinned under a heavy slab of ice. That was a stupid, crazy thing to do, and I realized that I was getting way too close to the edge of something dangerous.

Moving on — staggering is a more appropriate word — I came to a point due east of Promontory Point. It was here, from the looks of it, that the river turned west, and with about five miles to go, the way should have been easy going on overflow ice all the way to the igloo and the kayak. It wasn't. I was blocked from the overflow ice by another stream that was leaving the river and heading southwest across what I came to call the delta, a huge, boggy area with scattered streams and ice flows covering an area estimated at about five miles north-south, and ten miles east-west. I decided to camp again, and wait (again) to see whether the stream volume would decrease so I could cross it. (It didn't so I couldn't.) I camped and lightened my pack.

Once again I reasoned that if this stream left the river, it had to rejoin it, so I decided to follow it. I know it was the long way around, but I didn't see an alternative. I was like Frodo walking to Mount Doom, getting smaller physically and mentally with each succeeding step. No giant lady spider was lying in wait, but there were marshes, fens, ice flows, small islands of spruce, and many, many small streams, easily crossed with my thigh-length rubber boots but still worrisome by their propensity. Early in the afternoon of the thirtieth, with the stream on my right, I encountered my personal *bete noire*, another stream on my left. The two streams met ahead of me. They were both too deep to wade with boots. There ensued an hour or more of indecision. What to do? I could undress and cross the stream on the right, and then force my way across several miles of delta to the overflow, which I could see lying like a raised white line against the background of distant mountains. Or I could take the stream on the left and reach the old riverbank, or escarpment, which led in a large, unbroken curve westward to my destination. I chose the latter. I hunted for and found what I thought was the best crossing point, a place where the stream split for a few hundred yards into two smaller channels. Because of the large amount of tannic acid it was carrying, I couldn't see the bottom, but I assumed it was less than

waist deep. So I stripped off boots, pants, socks, and long johns, which I carried in my left hand. With my rifle in my right hand, I stepped half naked into the stream, and to any human observer, of which there were none, disappeared from view.

The stream was deep and swift, the bottom and sides covered with ice. I was being swept rapidly downstream. I could not stand, and had it not been for a drooping willow bough which I was able to grasp with the same hand that held the rifle, I would have lost boots or gun, or perhaps my life. I was out of the water within seconds. Standing on the bank with water pouring out of the barrel of my rifle, my immediate thought was that if a grizzly suddenly appeared I was in serious trouble. I also thought that this was no longer a game. The Protestant Work Ethic could go to Hell. This was a life-threatening situation and I had better start thinking of it that way. I dried the gun and bullets as best as I could before I worried about my wet clothes. The temperature was in the forties but there was a chill west wind and later, I knew, it would drop below freezing. So I grabbed all my stuff, raced to the nearest isolated stand of spruce, and built a fire to dry me and my clothes.

That night I slept very little, trying to decide what to do and eventually concluding that I should return to my cabin, and wait to go out with Mike by boat. Then I couldn't sleep for worrying that by the time I returned, Mike might have already left. And I knew I couldn't face that river again by myself until it had become a normal river, and who knew when that would be.

I returned upriver in two days, covering what had taken three to go down, and getting lost and found periodically. Lost, I would wander in a panic until I spotted opposite-pointing boot tracks, knowing, unlike Robinson Crusoe, that these tracks were mine, the only human tracks on this entire section of the river.

Nearing the cabin on my return, I contemplated what an extremely ironic ending this trip would have if Mike had decided to leave earlier, and we had passed each other today while I was wandering through the woods away from the river. Not being specifically religious, I decided to cover the spectrum and prayed to River Gods, Boat Gods and Early Departure Gods that this not be so. When I stumbled to my cabin, dropped that albatross of a pack, and went to the point to look for Mike's boat, there it was! I stood there applauding, not knowing how else to respond.

I went immediately to Mike's, blathered incoherently the whole evil story, and as of this writing we will depart on the fourth.

If there is a lesson to this unhappy saga, it is a trite one: As a result of this venture I am a sadder but wiser man. Sad because this failure, and that's what it was, has stolen some of my youthful spirit, a commodity in such short supply I have had to ration it for years. And wiser because I am once again impressed with how little I know.

Day 262, June 2 (Low 40, High 65, sunny)
According to KOTZ, Kotzebue (as quoted by Mike because my radio quit working on the day of my abortive exit), "sunrise today was at 3 a.m.; sunset will be next July 9, 39 days from now."

After talking with John about river conditions, Mike has decided we will now leave on the fifth. That's OK by me. Tomorrow I'm going to carve a canoe paddle.

Day 263, June 3 (Low 40, High 65, clear)
Six caribou were out front on the river bar this morning, two yearlings and four bulls. John said only bulls have been going by.

Late this afternoon I walked out to the point just as two wolves swam the river chasing a small herd of caribou, which had apparently also just crossed the channel. The caribou ran a few hundred yards downstream and recrossed the river. So did the wolves. This went on back and forth downriver until they were lost from sight. About an hour later one of the wolves returned looking very ragged and tired, obviously an unsuccessful hunter. On closer inspection the "wolf" turned out to be Sparkle, one of Mike's sled dogs. Now that they are not working, he lets them run loose part of each day. When we go downriver the six dogs he still has here will run along the shore part of the way. That's the theory. But, based on what I saw today, if they spot caribou. . . .

A very warm day. At midnight the river has risen a foot or more. That should help clear the ice downstream.

Day 264, June 4 (Low 40, High 60, clear)
River running, snow melting. Waiting to go. Stasis doesn't cut it. Feeling retroactive, even if the first birch leaves are popping out today.

Day 265, June 5 The Final, (Low 40, High 65, clear)
Today we go out, the Gods willing.

Day 266, June 6 (Low 40, High 65, clear)
Well, yes. The Gods were willing, but with some reluctance. Yesterday we started down running the dogs partway along the shore, then putting them all aboard when we saw caribou up ahead. Everything looked clear and easy until we reached Promontory Point, where we began to encounter heavy ice. The channel became narrower, the current faster and heavier, and the walls of ice on each side higher. Looming. Suddenly, without warning, we came around a tight corner and were swept under a huge shelf of ice. Both Mike and I were knocked out of the boat but we managed to hold onto the side. Two dogs were swept overboard. The boat was filling with water and threatening to capsize. The force of the water was scraping the boat deeper and deeper under the ice and farther downstream. I remember Mike yelling, "Stay with the boat! Stay with the boat!" Luckily the channel made another sharp turn at this point and the boat popped back out into the main stream. By some kind of miracle Mike and I, without speaking, crawled back into the boat from opposite sides in what amounted to a perfect balancing act. After several frantic tries Mike managed to start the motor just as we saw that the entire river was vanishing into a massive jumble of ice about a hundred yards below us. We headed slowly upstream against a very powerful current and stopped briefly at a gravel bar, where the two dogs thrown out by the impact had managed to swim. We were in a very narrow channel, like a deep ditch about twenty feet wide with walls of ice higher than our heads. Mike grabbed each dog and literally threw them up onto the ice.

Our intention was to go back upstream where the ice walls were lower, where we could beach the canoe and change to dry clothing. Just as the last dog was heaved up onto the ice, a monstrous block of ice, bigger than a house, came downriver revolving slowly. We were helpless. Had the ice hit us it would have smashed the canoe into splinters, and us along with it. As it passed us it revolved in the only way it could without hitting us. At about this time Mike asked whether I wanted to be boosted up with the dogs, an offer I was sorely tempted to accept, but didn't.

As we headed upstream dodging ice blocks, it was very tense going until the channel widened, the banks of ice lowered, and eventually we reached a spot where we could beach the canoe. After changing into dry clothes, we off-loaded a heavy tool chest, the motor and cans of gasoline, and then pushed, pulled, carried, and with the help of the dogs, now in harness, towed the canoe across four or five miles of ice, and five hours later arrived at Doug and Christy's. Today Mike and Doug are taking the dogs out with a sled to bring the motor and other abandoned gear back off the ice before they become part of breakup.

The river is ice-jammed below us, so we are stuck here for a few more days. As I write this, looking back the way we had come yesterday, I can see huge geysers of water exploding high above the ice, marking where the walls of ice are collapsing into the river. This is happening almost exactly in the area where we were swept under the ice.

138

Afterword

We were forced to wait five days for the river to clear enough for us to travel on it safely. Finally, on June 11, we headed downriver and arrived in the village without incident. I said goodbye to Mike and his dogs, flew to Kotzebue by light plane, caught a jet to Anchorage and a train from there to Denali National Park, and reported to work two weeks late. Since my return I have often been asked two questions: Why did I go up there? Depending upon my state of mind at the time the question is asked, I have a variety of answers, but the one I have come to use most often is a quote from Henry David Thoreau: "If a man does not keep pace with his companions, perhaps he is hearing a different drummer." The other question is, "Would I ever go back up there?" The answer is an unequivocal yes.

An Arctic Shopping List

6 boxes kitchen matches
50 lbs. white flour
25 lbs. whole wheat flour
5 lbs. cornmeal
5 lbs. masa harina
1 lb. rye flour
20 lbs. granulated sugar
1 lb. powdered sugar
5 lbs. brown sugar
5 lbs. honey
1 lb. molasses
1 lb. yeast
1 lb. baking powder
2 cans baking soda
2 lbs. salt
1 #10 powdered eggs
10 lbs. powdered milk
2 lbs. powdered buttermilk
1 #10 powdered cream
12 5.5-oz. cans milk
1 pkg. yogurt culture
2 gal. Wesson oil
2 #10 Crisco
10 lbs. butter
10 lbs. margarine
1 #10 peanut butter
10 lbs. Cheddar cheese
5 lbs. Mozzarella cheese
1 lb. Parmesan cheese
2 lbs. Jack cheese
4 8-oz. cream cheese
variety Cup-of-Soups
2 8-oz. vanilla
1 can pepper
2 cans cinnamon
1 pkg. minced onion
1 pkg. garlic powder
1 pkg. garlic salt

1 pkg. allspice
1 pkg. curry powder
1 pkg. ground cloves
2 bottles Worcestershire sauce
1 #10 freeze-dried soup (veg)
3 lbs. alfalfa seeds
1 lb. mung bean seeds
1 pkg. sunflower seeds
5 lbs. popcorn
5 lbs. lentils
2 lbs. barley
1 lb. blackeyed peas
5 lbs. brown rice
5 boxes instant grits
1 case canned ham
6 cans bacon, 1 side bacon
2 boxes dried hash browns
5 lbs. white rice
10 lbs. navy beans
3 lbs. pinto beans
2 lbs. kidney beans
2 lbs. lima beans
3 lbs. split peas
1 lb. wheat germ
1 lb. oatmeal
1 lb. walnuts
1 lb. almonds
1 lb. cashews
1 #10 can mixed nuts
1 #10 can peanuts
variety of teas
4 jars Maxim coffee
1 large Ovaltine
2 large hot chocolate
1 lb. baking chocolate
1 lb. coconut (shredded)
1 pkg. malted milk
2 lbs. semisweet choc-chip
2 large pkgs. M&M's

2 lbs. dried prunes
2 lbs. raisins
2 lbs. dates
1 #10 freeze-dried apples
1 #10 apple sauce
1 lb. dried apricots
1 #10 freeze-dried peaches
1 #10 freeze-dried strawberries
1 #10 pears
2 pints strawberry jam
2 pints raspberry jam
2 pints peach preserves
5 lbs. noodles
5 lbs. spaghetti
5 lbs. dried potatoes
1 #10 instant mashed potatoes
3 cans mushrooms
4 cans tuna
2 cans green chilis
4 cans olives
6 cans corn
4 boxes tapioca
6 boxes instant Jiffy cornbread
6 cans tomato sauce
12 cans tomato paste
4 cans apple pie filling
2 cans blueberry filling
2 large bottles ketchup
2 large bottles vinegar
1 gal. olive oil
1 qt. mustard
1 qt. pickles
2 jars mayonnaise
1 large bottle lemon juice
6 cans tomatoes
1 #10 Tang
1 #10 lemonade
variety puddings and Jello
2 boxes saltine crackers

2 boxes pilot bread
1 large waxed paper
2 large foil wrap
1 Saran Wrap
6 instant macaroni and cheese
1 gal. maple syrup
variety dry cereal
10 lbs. pancake mix
5 lbs. Bisquick
2 bottles salsa (hot)
2 bottles soy sauce
3 cans pineapple
1 sourdough starter
2 large Quaker oats
12 rolls toilet paper
soap (hand, dish, laundry)
1 #10 freeze-dried cottage cheese
1 lb. mincemeat
cream of tartar
marshmallows
kitchen sponge
1 Aladdin lamp, 6 mantles
2 chimneys, 3 wicks
3 Eagle kerosene lamp chimneys
20 gal. kerosene
3 36-inch saw blades
1 double-bladed ax
2 12-volt fencer batteries
4x15 feet Mylar
4x6-feet-x-4-inch foam rubber
20-foot-wide roll of 6 mil
    Visqueen
2 tubes silicone seal
1 can furnace cement
1 sharpener stone
3 sections 6-inch galvanized
    stovepipe
1 can camping fuel
staples and staple gun

A Record of Winter Reading in the Arctic

White Dawn, James Houston
The Palace Guard, Dan Rather
Daiyimo, a corporation of flacks
The Good Shepherd, C.S. Forester
A Tale of Two Cities, Charles Dickens
The Tamarind Seed, Evelyn Anthony
Kidnapped, Robert Louis Stevenson
Rabbit Boss, Thomas Sanchez
50 Great Short Stories, edited by Milton Crane
Doors, Ezra Hannon
Amazon, Roy Sparkia
The Starship and the Canoe, Kenneth Brower
Adventures of a Red Sea Smuggler, Henry de Montfreid
The Autobiography of Malcom X
Shadow of the Hunter, Richard K. Nelson
Triple, Ken Follett
The Dancing Wu Li Masters, Gary Zukav
Death of a Fool, Ngaio Marsh
Killer in the Rain, Raymond Chandler
Never Cry Wolf, Farley Mowat
Shike; I, *Time of the Dragons;* II, *Last of the Zinja*, Robert Shea
The Elephant Man, Christine Sparks
Falconer, John Cheever
The Firmament of Time, Loren Eiseley
A Study in Scarlet, Sir Arthur Conan Doyle
The Valdez Horses, Lee Hoffman
Anthem, Ayn Rand
The Partners, Louis Auchincloss
The Man, Irving Wallace
The Tracker, Tom Brown, Jr.
Thoreau: Walden & Other Writing, Henry David Thoreau
All The President's Men, Bernstein & Woodward
The Godfather, Mario Puzo
Tai-Pan, James Clavell
The Final Days, Woodward & Bernstein
The Thin Man, Dashiell Hammett
Moscow Coach, Philip McCutchan
Serpico, Peter Maas

Fatal Vision, Joe McGinnis
Trinity, Leon Uris
The Implosion Conspiracy, Louis Nizer
Journal of a Trapper, 1834-1843, Osborne Russell
The Long Walk, Slavomir Rawicz
The Uses of Enchantment, Bruno Bettelheim
The Last Great Race, Tim Jones
Stillwell and the American Experience in China, Barbara Tuchman
Saint Jack, Paul Theroux
Fire in the Lake, Frances FitzGerald
Zen Bhuddhism, D.T. Suzuki
The Barking Deer, Jonathan Rubin
Aztec, Gary Jennings
Tinker, Tailor, Soldier, Spy, John Le Carre
The Honourable Schoolboy, John Le Carre
Mister God, This is Anna, Fynn
Nunaga, Duncan Pryde
The Milagro Beanfield War, John Nichols
Armageddon, Leon Uris
The Rising Sun, John Toland
Titus Groan, The Gormenchast Trilogy #1, Mervyn Peake
Art and Illusion, E.H. Gombrich
Annapurna, Maurice Herzog
Sirens, Eric Van Lustbader
The Bourne Identity, Robert Ludlum
American Caesar—Douglas MacArthur, William Manchester
The Word, Irving Wallace
Trade Winds, M.M. Kaye
War and Peace, Leo Tolstoy
Kiowa Fires, Donald Porter
The Big Sky, A.B. Guthrie
Watership Down, Richard Adams
The Civil War in Spain, 1936-39, edited by Robert Payne
The 9th Directive, Adam Hall
The Virginian, Owen Wister
The Great Railway Bazaar, Paul Theroux
Hitler, A Study in Tyranny, Allan Bullock
A Man Called Intrepid, William Stevenson
The Last Ranger, Zane Grey

Passenger to Frankfurt, Agatha Christie
Refiner's Fire, Mark Helprin
The Gulag Archipelago, Aleksandr I. Solzhenitsyn
The Magic Journey, John Nichols
Explorations in Alaska, George M. Stoney
Paradigms Lost, John Simon
QB VII, Leon Uris
Mark Twain's Best, Samuel Clemens
The Holcroft Covenant, Robert Ludlum
The Mosquito Coast, Paul Theroux
The Plague, Albert Camus
Cromwell, Antonia Frazer
The Book of Daniel, E.L. Doctorow
From Where the Sun Now Stands, Will Henry
Nirvana Blues, Paul Nichols
The Boy Who Invented The Bubble Gun, Paul Gallico
Coming Into The Country, John McPhee
The Universe at Large, Hermann Bondi
Far Tortuga, Peter Matthiessen
Selected Poems, Robinson Jeffers
My Life With the Eskimos, Vilhjalmur Stefansson

MORE OUTDOOR LORE..is available through the many other books published by Alaska Northwest. We offer the first-hand accounts of big-game guides, field guides, camp cookbooks, and much more. Ask for these books at your favorite bookstore, or contact Alaska Northwest for a complete catalog.

ALASKA NORTHWEST BOOKS™
A Division of GTE Discovery Publications, Inc.
130 Second Avenue South, Edmonds, WA 98020
Call toll-free 1-800-331-3510

WILDERNESS SURVIVAL GUIDE
How to build snow shelters, cross icy rivers, and build your own survival gear.
$9.95 ($12.95 in Canada)
106 pages / paperback original / 5 3/8 by 8 5/8 inches
ISBN 0-88240-317-6

ALASKA BEAR TALES
These remarkable true accounts of encounters with bears will stay with you long after you've finished the book. Whether you're a resident of the Far North or dwell in the Lower 48, ALASKA BEAR TALES will grab you and keep you reading.
$10.95 ($13.90 in Canada)
318 pages / paperback original / 5 3/8 by 8 3/8 inches
ISBN 0-88240-232-2

ALASKA SOURDOUGH
ALASKA SOURDOUGH is an indispensable addition to your cookbook collection. More than 95 recipes — everything from hotcakes to doughnuts — show the versatility of this Alaskan frontier staple.
$6.95 ($88.85 in Canada)
190 pages / paperback original / 7 5/16 by 9 inches
ISBN 0-88240-085-1

ALASKA WILD BERRY GUIDE AND COOKBOOK
A field guide and cookbook that will delight the eye and the palate! Gorgeous drawings help you identify the berries. The recipes show you how to turn your finds into scrumptious treats everyone will enjoy. A great gift for the whole family.
$14.95 ($18.95 in Canada)
201 pages / paperback original / 6 by 9 inches
ISBN 0-88240-229-3